SAMARA BEND

Travels in Russia

Illustrated

Edward Dyas

Note to Reader.

Samara Bend is the name given to a sweeping curve of the Volga River where it circles the majestic Zhiguli Hills. It is where this story begins.

Personal names have been changed within this book for privacy.

CONTENTS

ISBN: 9781074693190

SAMARA BEND

Since youth Russia had intrigued me, its art, literature, music, incomprehensible ways, enormous diversity, turbulent often directionless history and its eternal sadness. It is a land, I thought, of self-destructive despair.

Most people have an opinion of Russia gathered from a media that portrays it as the bad guy of the northern hemisphere, and some have a preconceived idea drawn from classic novels, films or Sunday journalism and it is as inaccurate as a shard or fragment of a giant mosaic that conveys a story but a story nothing like the whole.

I began with my view of Russia accumulated from history books, ballet, music and novels. Even though I had never been there I thought I had a good idea of what this beautiful, romantic, yet cold hearted nation was like. My views were not based upon experience and that was about to change.

It began with a glorious summer day as I stared from my office window. It had been an uneventful year, of work, monotony, and boredom. I suddenly knew I had to get away. An impetuous decision to do something different came over me, a desire to run away without telling anyone, to go somewhere I had never been, perhaps spend six months travelling, become an international, unambitious, drifter, whose only goal was to turn wandering into a way of life. With that in mind, and an impulse I couldn't deny, I decided to set off, alone, without an itinerary.

The sun bleached Mediterranean seemed as good a place as any to begin, cloudless skies, relaxing indolence, a flotsam of what had once been a fulcrum of history between north and south, east and west, the very place where civilisation began.

Thinking over this quixotic phantasy what better place to begin, I reasoned, than the sun blistering Island of Rhodes where a great Colossus once stood depicting the Sun God Helios, 108 feet tall and as high as the Statue of Liberty.

A Travel Agent told me, 'Go north of Faliraki' where there were good, under crowded, beautiful beaches and hotels, out of range of frenetic summer teenage revellers whom I was told tended to populate round the bars to the south. A five star hotel with a beach front was suggested. Within a few weeks I gave in my notice and set off determined to leave all my yesterdays behind, like leaving years of baggage in lost luggage at an airport.

This wasn't the first time I had done this. At the age of 17 years, with both my parents dead and when hardly fending for myself, on life's bumpy road, I was working in a legal department of a large transport company. The RAF had rejected me at a medical due to a sudden asthma attack that never returned after that day. I had tried to join the RAF to add adventure to my young life. Once, at fifteen years, I read about a lone yachtsman and had written to him to take me on his thirty five footer, circumnavigating the globe, but he never replied. Probably a good thing because one day they found him stabbed to death, by an unknown assailant, in a run-down Paris flat.

So at 17yrs I just left my job and took to the road and worked anywhere, at anything, staying in expensive hotels when I could and shabby lodging houses when I couldn't, until my money ran out. Then I hitchhiked to somewhere else.

My greatest asset was youth; people I met seemed to like my courage and enthusiasm and wanted to help.

Now here I was years later, with confidence born of some experience, setting off in the words of George Herbert, 'Free as the road and loose as the wind'.

So another adventure began.

The taxi idled between a long avenue of trees that led to a tropical hotel entrance. Inside the foyer, cool in the oppressive summer heat, I paused and gazed around. It was quiet, almost deserted, except for a desk clerk and a woman with her back to me browsing maps and leaflets on a revolving book display. The hotel appearance was of a tropics 19th century club of the Raj, cane chairs, glass topped tables, cool marble floors, exotic plants and a male desk clerk, standing at attention. Before approaching the clerk, I glanced at the woman, browsing the leaflets. Elegantly tall she was dressed in white cotton slacks and short, loose blouse tied at the waist, her light brown hair, clasped with painted brooch, fell down her perfectly straight back as she stood poised, weight on one foot, like a ballet dancer.

Refusing the porter's help with my luggage I checked in and was led to a first floor room with spectacular view overlooking the sea. The scene from the window was landscaped lawns, swimming pool, and beyond them, canopied tables. Further out a boardwalk ran the length of a golden beach racing along a curving coastline of a bay enclosed by distant hills.

After showering I flopped down till evening shrank its August 32C temp then walked to a nearby ramshackle village, past bars and uninspiring shops before returning early to laze beside the hotel swimming pool. Walking down a shaded tree lined avenue to the hotel, I noticed ahead of me the beautiful brunette I had first noticed in the hotel foyer. Now she was accompanied by a girl of about fourteen years.

'Hello,' I greeted as I caught up with them.

'Hello! Are you English?' the Brunette stopped to ask, looking closely at me.

'Yes.' I slowed to walk beside them.

'Are you at our hotel? I thought I saw you there,' she asked.

'I am. I arrived today.'

The woman, in her thirties, was truly beautiful. She held out her hand. 'My name is Galina. This is my daughter Katya. You must excuse me my English is not good.'

Her daughter coldly looked me over without a smile or hello.

Galina's eyes were a dark brown oval above high round cheek bones.

'You are on holiday? Galina asked.

'Yes, one week.'

'We too, we arrived yesterday?

'We are Russian,' the unsmiling teenager said in perfect English. 'Have you been to Russia?' she asked as though admonishing me.

'No.'

'How old are you?' she asked. Later I learned that this was one of the first questions Russians ask, when they meet someone for the first time, very much the way the English say, 'Lovely day'.

Our conversation led to easy friendship as we walked together and in the hotel foyer, over a glass of wine, we agreed to visit together the historic walled City of Rhodes. From that time on we were constant companions. Galina told me her husband, a qualified Master Builder, was away working on a large construction project in Cyprus. She'd been alone for months missing him every day but her work in a Russian bank and her daughter's needs kept her fully occupied. Galina dressed seductively, her slacks of white cotton left little to reveal and on beaches she wore a micro bikini. I was to learn this was a common trend among Russian women who since the end of Communism, with their new independence, try to emulate images of Hollywood celebrities and Russian women believe themselves superior to any women alive.

I hired a car and drove the three of us around the Island and then for one week we were inseparable. On sweltering evenings we swam or played a Russian card game Katya said was called 'Idiot'. Needless to say she beat me every time but I took consolation that no one could beat Katya. If this game had been on tables in Las Vegas she would have made a fortune.

The Mediterranean attracts large numbers of Russian holiday makers. Cruise ships often have a majority of Russian passengers who have become so prosperous, in 'New Russia', they take three holidays overseas per annum. In the Soviet era they were inescapably trapped within their country but now it is easy to obtain visas, providing ones income is above an average level.

The hotel I was at had a good number of Russian tourists. Galina introduced me to a family, from Minsk, that she'd met there. The husband owned a successful business creating and constructing exhibition stalls for international centres all over Europe.

'I often set up exhibitions in England,' he told me, 'and frequently visit London and Birmingham.' He preferred Russia under Putin.

He was the only Russian male I saw at the hotel but I counted eight Russian women there, with their children, all walking with upright stanch and all of athletic build and each morning the hotel gym was used by them more than anyone else. Galina rose at 6.00 am each day to run three miles along the beach boardwalk followed by a swim in the sea for one hour. Often I noticed

Russians engaging in stretching exercises, at all times of day, along the beach front. I couldn't help but compare them to L.A. Californians but with a noticeable difference Russians, highly sociable, often sat in close friendship at beach front tables laughing and drinking together and anyone was welcome. Individually they are self-possessed, thoughtful in their replies, with a quiet natural dignity in their demeanour.

The day came for Galina and Kate to leave so I helped carry their bags to a waiting taxi.

'You email us?' Galina asked. 'Maybe you can visit us in Russia?'

'Maybe,.' I replied.

They waved goodbye, Katya staring out of the taxi window, still unsure what to make of me, until they were out of sight.

Returning home to England, to organise finances, and put under wraps my normal, uneventful routine life, I searched a library for information on Samara, the Russian city where Galina and Kate lived. Most Russian travel books didn't even mention it nor recent publications except for a sentence or two. Considering Samara is the sixth largest city in Russia this puzzled me. I discovered the city was missing from most Atlases. In only one book did I come across a reference to it, in a casual paragraph, that said "A city beside the Volga River that began as a 16th Century Trading Station on a part of the Volga known as Samara Bend."

The name intrigued me, 'Samara Bend.' It had a ring of destiny in it like a Hemingway novel. I knew immediately, instinctively, this was no ordinary city and was a place I had to see.

For one month I journeyed three hours per week to a distant language centre to learn Russian at the only college teaching the subject. At home I did my best to speed up the process with books and tapes. At the language centre I learned a major difference between English and Russians, a personality chasm reflected in the Russian language itself, Russians are bluntly direct to the point of impoliteness.

It was a small class of about six people; not many English want to learn Russian. The course tutor introduced herself as Tatiana. Several weeks into the course I asked if we could address her as Tanya.

Tatiana flared up, 'No, in Russia you must know a person for three years before using an abbreviation of their name. You must always call me Tatiana.' She raised her arm in a sweeping gesture above her head like a ballerina about to make a grandiose bow, 'Tatiana is such a beautiful, poetic sounding name,' she told us.

Russian language also reveals the cultural directness of the Slavic mind, with nothing of the over-polite, diplomatic frills, of English and it emphasises personal pride and dignity.

While all this was going on, one day I received an email from Galina suggesting I come to Samara at any time to suit me. She would be working at the bank but her daughter Katya and her husband's parents would accompany me during the day.

The Russian Tourist Office in London arranged a visa and flight. Their agent warned me I would need an interpreter while in Samara. He seemed surprised I wanted to go there.

'This city is not a tourist venue. Very few people speak fluent English there,' he said.

'I need a long term visa' I requested.

'The most you will be allowed is six months and we need details of all places you will be staying at before you go.'

'I can't do that as I am not sure which cities I will travel to.'

'In that case you can't be given a visa,' he said abruptly.

This was my first acquaintance with incomprehensible Russian bureaucracy.

'Is there no way round this?' I asked unable to conceal my disappointment.

'Obtain a letter from the people you are visiting to assure us you will be staying with them. They will be responsible for you while in Russia. This might work but there is no certainty.'

I contacted Galina who informed me her father in law had been a Soviet politician and was now a successful 'New Russian'. This meant a variety of things, but generally indicated he was an entrepreneur of influence with police and government and, as in all countries, that made all the difference.

Back at the Russian Travel Agency I explained who my Russian friends were. The agent fell silent before ringing several numbers then began the process of looking at my passport and the address given. Before presenting me with a visa he asked me ominously, 'Are you really going to do this?'

'Yes,' I replied.

'Take care,' he warned kindly but ambiguously.

At Heathrow there were no long queues to board the Russian Aeroflot flight to Moscow's Sheremetevo airport. The flight was on time, the flight attendant's surly. Stern, unsmiling, unfriendliness seems to go with all official duty in Russia and it is a facade much like wearing a suit to the office.

My seat was central aisle. As I settled into my place I saw a heavily built Russian woman, to my right across the aisle, looking as though she could have taken on the whole British army single handed, asking her fellow passenger if she would exchange her seat, so she could have an aisle seat. The young Russian beside her calmly but coldly refused so this formidable epitome of all Russian matriarchs leaned over towards me and asked if she could have my aisle seat.

In Greek mythology fate holds sway even over God himself. Everyone has experienced these unpredictable moments, for good or ill, and this was to be one of those moments. Being English and by nature an over polite super co-operator I agreed to help this heavy boned mother of all the Russia's and politely took her seat, across the gangway, at the window. Weary with travel I just wanted to close my eyes and sleep.

Well into the flight I began to notice the determined young woman sitting beside me. She seemed about eighteen years, intriguingly beautiful, with sophisticated, intelligent face, light brown hair and violet coloured, humorous eyes.

'Are you going to Moscow?' I asked.

'No. Yaroslavl, but I will have to catch a train in Moscow,' she replied turning her magnificent eyes to scrutinise me. 'You are English?'

'Absolutely.'

'How old are you?' The usual first question Russians ask. She spoke with a Russian accent but faultless English.

'Does it matter? I will still be the same person afterwards.'

She smiled, 'No'.

'Let me guess your age, I would say eighteen, maybe twenty?' I queried.

The young woman laughed.

'Well I have a twelve years old daughter. I'm thirty three.'

This broke any reservations we had about each other. Her name was Svetlana.

She was not only beautiful but Dean of a Russian University and had been in London doing research. Before we parted in Moscow she gave me her email, home address and phone number and we agreed to meet in England next time she was there.

Later I discovered the address she had given me was not her own but that of a friend of hers. It was something else I had to learn about Russians, in spite of their sociability, they trust no one.

Svetlana said goodbye at Moscow's Sheremetyevo 2 airport and I caught a taxi to Sheremetyevo 1, an adjoining airport, that accommodates all domestic flights. The design of Moscow airport is unusual in that two airports, which are in fact separate, successfully share the same runways. Very few airports in the world use such a system yet it is a superior method of border control and monitor of passengers. Since my visit another Moscow airport Domodedovo has been massively extended to cater mostly for business flights.

Western media rarely speak of Putin's presidency in positive terms. In reality modernisation programmes within Russia, under his leadership, have no equal in the world. What I saw later, during my travels within Russia, was new airports, magnificent new railway stations, vast new shopping centres, restoration of Tsarist monuments and palaces, revitalised universities and improved standards of living. Average monthly wages have risen eight fold during Putin's presidency and GDP by more than that. These are verifiable statistics yet Western media mostly concentrates on the less fortunate aspects of Russian life. Of course not all Russians have been able to enjoy this new prosperity. There is large scale corruption within Russia's economy and no one, not even Putin, has ever been able to overcome this Russian scourge. When you consider the enormous size and complexity of the country it is understandable why Russia could never survive without a strong autocrat commanding all from one seat of power.

The departure lounge of Sheremetyevo 1, which at this time was a shabby, shed like structure, reminded me of a Railway waiting room. Putin hadn't got round to modernising it yet but was in the process. I thought it like a stopping off place before some notorious incarceration in a remote Gulag which at one time it had been.

A family of Russians, noticing my unease, for some reason took me under their wing. They spoke little English but managed to tell me they came from a small village close to my destination of Samara. This was my first, but not last, experience of Russians protecting English tourists.

Russian press is full of stories of tourists being robbed and murdered, that does happen, but it's true of all countries not only Russia. No doubt tourists alone in Russia are an easy prey and eventually do meet thieves, unscrupulous traders, corrupt police and customs, but so do native Russians, not just tourists, and I doubt if it is any worse than any other part of the world. I have seen and experienced violence and criminality in America and Britain and Australia far in excess of anything I experienced in Russia. What I found was Russians are among the most welcoming people to be found anywhere. I felt safe among them. Hospitality there has a timeless tradition, born of days when travellers through its tortured, frozen, unimaginable, emptiness survived only if every family made their home places of hospitable refuge.

At a dingy, airport lounge, stall I purchased coffee and was charged three times more than the Russians around me. The woman serving me did it with guilt in her eyes. I supposed she had no choice so I said nothing. Foreigners in Russia, even when married to Russians, or have lived there for years, are charged two or three times more than locals and this extortionate practice is especially true of services under State control.

Russians mostly admire the English.. This admiration can be traced back as far as Elizabethan England and was noticeable in both Peter the Great and Catherine. Often Russians gave me concessions, and preferential treatment, that was denied other foreign tourists.

The Russian family befriending me, at Moscow's airport, were determined to stay with me until I boarded our flight to Samara. Roughly dressed they were obviously poor. At their feet lay huge cardboard boxes, tied with string, bound with parcel tape, filled with items purchased in Turkey for resale in their village. This type of trade, common throughout Russia, is a tradition that goes back to the gigantic medieval fairs held in Petersburg, Moscow and Samara. These enormous annual markets, trading on the frozen rivers of Russia's huge, diverse empire, were the largest in the world.

Istanbul, where my airport friends had visited for their purchases, boasts one of the largest Russian settlements, outside of Russia, created solely to handle this daily trade in goods. Istanbul's Russian quarter has grown into a sizeable town, filled with shops, restaurants, shipping companies, accountants, international solicitors and oligarch money laundering offices where activities are easily hidden within this lucrative trade.

By the time I caught my flight to Samara it was already late and dark. The small Aeroflot jet was noisy, smelling of fuel, was rickety, aged and tired. It gave an impression of being found on a battlefield after 1945. Boxes, bundles and bags, lay loosely, inconveniently and unsafely, everywhere. No attempt could be made to secure items in overhead lockers nor was any effort made to restrict weight.

Choosing a window seat I watched an endlessly, lonely landscape of forest and night disappearing below. It was like viewing some vast, lost universe. This claustrophobic darkness was broken only occasionally by isolated clusters of village lights flash of river or lake. The mysterious, black distance between these isolated communities made me wonder how they survived, yet they always did, and had done so for a millennia.

It was impossible to sleep. A draught of cold air, from some unknown source, tugged at my legs constantly. We were all relieved when eventually the aircraft arrived at Samara's Kurumoch Airport at 1.00 am in the bleakly silent hours of morning.

Galina was already there. Taking my arm, she led me to meet a tall, heavy boned, robustly fit looking Russian. His blue eyes smiling, his close cropped grey hair giving him dignified authority, he stood beside his black, Japanese, four wheel drive.

'This is my father in law, Sasha.' Galina introduced.

'Menya zavoot Edward. Kak Dyela,' I greeted.

Surprised at being addressed in Russian he took my hand and smiling answered, 'Kharasho, ochen preeyatna.'

Samara's Kurumoch airport, isolated, looked like a warehouse deliberately hidden in the landscape. During Soviet times it had been built purposely difficult to reach and coldly unwelcoming. It was fifty six kilometres from Samara city. Its bleak appearance dampened my eagerness to be there. I began wondering what I would find, for good or ill, in this city about which I could find so little information. Until 1990, and the end of Communism, Samara had been closed to the outside world, due to its technology and missile based industries, and that was why the airport was built so secretly hidden and forbidding.

Sasha (Russian diminutive for Alexander and Alexandra) helped lift my suitcase and holdall into his vehicle. We drove through a pitch night, over potholed roads narrow as English country lanes. All we could see, for ages, was dense, overgrown, forest through which our vehicle swerved from side to side as Sasha did his best to avoid the worst of the crumbling highway. Above was no moon or jewel stars just a heavy leafy sky. Galina clung to my arm, in generous gesture of assurance, and no doubt for her own safety. The roads became better maintained as we reached the city outskirts. When at last we reached Samara I was too weary to note any first impressions. Sasha drove us to a large complex of luxurious blocks of flats. Russia has many, poorly constructed, worker, high rise flats but the ones we arrived at had been built for the Soviet elite, factory directors, politicians and KGB.

The door to Galina's flat, encased in steel, needed three keys to open it. Inside the flat the door was padded with puckered red leather. A woman of around sixty years, welcomed us inside. She introduced herself enthusiastically as Olga, Sasha's wife, and had come to welcome me. She was stout, happy, and short, with flashing gold teeth that she was embarrassed about when she smiled. The rooms were large with high ceilings. I put down my cases in an enormous living room lined with teak panelling and a floor to ceiling bookcase. Every window had shutters and were double glazed. The outside wall was 18 inches thick and the room lit by a three feet diameter crystal chandelier.

This wasn't anything like the cramped, downtrodden, dingy flats I had seen in numerous television documentaries of the way most Russians lived. Beyond the living salon were two spacious bedrooms. There was a wide kitchen with dining table in the centre and room for six people to dine. Russians being notoriously sociable their kitchens become a centre of gossip, argument and revelry.

Opening my suitcase I presented Sasha and Olga with a boxed gift of two wine glasses, engraved with their names Olga and Sasha, exact replicas of glasses made for the Captain's cabin of the Titanic, made by the same company that had produced all of the glassware for that tragic liner. Inside the box I had slipped a card that said, 'Don't go down with the Ship.'

Later that same day Olga stopped by with a gift for me, an exquisitely decorated Russian Samovar so large I wondered how on earth I would be able to carry it when I left.

Samara always had settlements, along the banks of its massive Volga River. Excavations have revealed a culture at least 7000 years old. Italian cartographers had shown Samara on maps in the 14th century. Its fame, as port and city, however didn't begin in earnest until 16th century traders began to appreciate its ideal and beautiful setting at the confluence of the Volga and Samara Rivers. It soon became prosperous, a commercial station with fortifications and a boundary between Christian Russia and the untameable nomadic tribes invading from the Steppes. Trade through Samara's port came from all parts of Asia. Persians came, as did Byzantium, using the wide and gentle Volga to transport their goods to a growing Russian Empire and this lovely city. It must have been a truly magnificent sight, the broad Volga filled with ships, barges, and men of all races, calling in foreign voices, bargaining their wares along its colourful river wharves.

In winter, when the river froze, the Volga was transformed into a gigantic international market of tents, brilliantly decorated marquees, sleds, troikas and skiers. These great annual fairs attracted visitors from all over Europe as well as Asia. Some caravans, from remote parts, could take as much as one year to arrive. To that imagine the varied, splendid colours and designs of Russian dress, interspersed among bearded, kaftan robed, exotic merchant travellers from Asia and one gets some idea of these wonderful trading fairs that continued until the October Revolution of 1917 swept them all away like snow in the wind.

You need to see the Volga to understand why this river is called 'The Mother of Russia' and at first sight I fell in love with it.

On my first day in Samara I woke to a glorious sunny morning, of light streaming through   delicate pink curtains, filling my room with a sunrise of red and gold. From the bedroom window I could see lawned gardens and mature trees.

The bedroom door opened and in walked Galina.

'Would you like   coffee or tea?   Perhaps egg on toast?'

Galina wearing white silk blouse and cotton slacks was alert and crisp.

'Let me shave first?' I asked.

'Very un- Russian' she smiled, 'Of course.' She showed me the bathroom and said, 'The toilet is in a separate room.'

Russians separate bathroom and toilet, due to their once communal living, but since the end of Communism they are changing that to a Western model.

Over coffee Galina said, 'I have asked for two weeks off so I can spend time with you. Until you know Russian better it isn't safe to be on your own and there is a lot to see.'

Galina's flat was close to Samara's Volga Embankment so after breakfast we climbed a long flight of steps that wound through parkland greenery, neatly mown lawns and luxuriant trees, with views overlooking the river. At the apex of this steep verdant hillside we could see the great expanse of the eternal river that has always been the creator and great artery of this endless country.

Though called the 'Mother of Russia' the Volga could just as readily be called the 'Mother of Europe' since it is the largest of all European Rivers traversing some 2,200 miles. It was along this river all those distant traders journeyed, from every quarter of Christian, Muslim and Jewish settlements to sell their wares. Its tranquil, broad grandeur and the rolling hills beyond captivated me.

Atop this hillside is a plateau named Slavy Square and on it a gigantic steel monument with a towering 40 metre high splinter pedestal representing a ray of light and on this, at its top, is a 13 metre figure holding stylised aeroplane wings above its head. It was all paid for by the workers of Samara in appreciation of their city's enormous achievement producing aircraft during World War 11.

'This is our "Monument of Glory," Galina explained. 'It represents our city and aeroplane engineers who worked here during the Second World War.'

Below this celebrated monument, facing the Volga for all to see, the name CAMARA proudly introduces this lovely city in a 42 metre proclamation.

The achievements of Russia's aviators, during World War 11, were without equal. During four years, of conflict, Samara's engineers turned out an incredible 35,000 aircraft, and a fighter squadron of 24 aeroplanes for every day of the year, an almost unbelievable display of Russia's unstoppable determination and tireless dedication, in their attempt to save their beloved Country.

You feel compelled to remove your hat with tears in your eyes.

From the Monument of Glory Galina led me to the great square, Ploshad Slavy, 'the Square of the Slavs', which is a war memorial plaza with the eternal flame you find in every Russian city.

Nowhere else is there such pride in war heroes as in Russia and with good reason. Though it has taken a long time to be acknowledged Western historians now agree that Hitler, like Napoleon before him, was defeated not by Europeans and their allies but by Russians, on the bloodthirsty soil of Mother Russia.

We sat down, in the summer sunshine, wearied by the climb. A bride and groom were having photos taken beside the war memorial, she in a pure white, floor length, folded bridal gown, with white flowers in her hair, the groom in dark suit and smiling, clean face.

Noticing my surprise Galina said, 'This is our way. We like to end wedding celebrations in the presence of our heroes, to say thank you, you made it possible for us.' They were saying to the fallen dead, we are still here and our happiness is because of you.

Love of nation is part of Russia's national psyche and so deeply ingrained there is no parallel anywhere in the West. Russians have, since the earliest days of their conversion to Christianity, believed in a Russian Soul. Since the fall of Communism, which had espoused Atheism, they have once more revived the belief in 'Holy Russia' which had always been there hidden in silence. From Ploshad Slavvy we strolled to the Volga Embankment and its litter free beaches of golden sand, volley ball courts and circular changing huts that looked like giant coca cola cans.

Out of curiosity I peered inside one of these changing huts expecting to find graffiti, cigarette butts and beer cans but instead discovered spotless interior, cleanly scrubbed rotund seats and neatly raked sand floor.

Beyond the beach the river flowed quietly indifferent to anything man could do to its tireless, irresistible journey, to the Caspian Sea.

Five and a half million years ago the Volga had flowed into an ocean, but then the Caspian for some reason became the largest landlocked lake on Earth and is now where this wonderful river meets its demise.

Samara's river promenade is skirted by meticulously groomed parks filled with perfect flower beds, trees and tidy lawns. Samara is a groomed and clean city Russians generally maintain their streets and parks with exceptional care. The only untidy one I ever saw was in Moscow's Gorky Park.

Along the embankment men in shorts, and bikini clad women, were roller blading down the long miles of the Volga shoreline. It reminded me of California's Santa Monica but not even there had I seen such beautiful women.

Samara, since the days of Katherine the Great, had attracted settlements of Germans known as 'Volga Germans'. They were religious, industrious communities who with their Germanic Protestant work ethic became successful businessmen but times change. In the Soviet era, especially under the dictatorship of Stalin, these prosperous Germans were humiliated and murdered. They, who had helped make Samara so successful, were now seen as despised bourgeoisie who had become wealthy on the struggling backs and sweat of the Russian people. These Volga Germans however have left a lasting genetic legacy. Other settlers had joined them from Bohemia, now the Czech Republic, to add to their racial mix. This drift of Germans and Western Slav, combined with Steppes Tatar, has produced a remarkable genetic strength, and beauty that is outstanding and I would say unsurpassed in any part of the world.

Western news and media had led me to expect Russian poverty, a down trodden people, struggling to recover from their Soviet past. No-one mentioned physical excellence, perfect parks, or the happy, successful, welcoming people I met there. Western media, in this respect, is completely false or deliberately disseminating fake news.

Along the length of the Volga embankment are bars that sprout alive in the evening with tables spread out in the sunshine and beside them brightly decorated marquees.

'We can come here later,' Galina smiled, 'It comes to life later.'

'It's lovely at the moment,' I enthused.

'It changes, late afternoon you will see people playing volley ball or swimming in the river. At sunset all these booths and bars open so then we walk the embankment.'

In the evening Sasha and Olga visited to walk with us beside the lively, Samara embankment. At 11.00 pm a large, perfect moon, in a cloudless diamond sky shone over the Eastern bank of the river. I could clearly see the wavy swirl of the Milky Way shining through the heavens like the Volga through the mystic landscape of the Steppes.

The embankment was flush with promenaders laughing beside the river and revelling in marquee entertainment and music. A pop group were singing in English, at another a bucking bronco tossed men and women, laughing, onto a mattress floor. Not one person completed the bronco ride but all those would be cowboys, to everyone's great amusement and cheers got back on for another try.

Sasha led us to an open air bar beside the embankment wall where we sat, and chatted, the evening away drinking local Zhiguli beer.

'Would you like a swim?' Sasha asked, using Galina's daughter Kate to interpret.

I glanced at my watch. It was 11.30 pm. 'I don't have trunks,' I apologised not enthused at the idea of swimming in an ice cold Volga.

A lifelong sportsman, Sasha put his hand in his pocket pulled out a pair of trunks and replied, 'On a warm evening always carry a pair of trunks.' He changed on the beach and swam in the moonlight at least a quarter mile from shore on the mile wide Volga, adjusting his angle of travel against the current so that when finished he returned to exactly the spot he had flung himself in.

Olga, once a Russian champion tennis player at 65 years was a heavily built, shy woman of kindly disposition. When she smiled, she displayed her shock of gold front teeth, and then realising they were out of fashion in modern Russia, habitually, quickly closed her lips hiding her innate, spontaneous, humour in embarrassment. Russian women habitually put on a brave, stoic face but in unguarded moments are perpetually sad, longing for male attention, love and protection.

Sasha was a successful businessman though I was never able to define exactly what he did. In communist days he had been a Soviet politician then with the rise of Capitalism began organising tennis tournaments internationally. This wasn't however his sole means of income. Like all Russian businessmen he never spoke of his work, nor would his family, who were all as silent about it as any Cosa Nostra brotherhood.

After the collapse of Communism many former politicians became wealthy executives, in large industrial companies, using their influence and Party contacts to obtain whatever work they found most lucrative legal or not.

On our way back from the embankment I noticed police cars, hidden among the trees, at every garden and park entrance.

'Tomorrow we go to our family Dacha.' Galina said.

'Do you like tennis?' Kate asked.

'I used to play, but not well. I'm out of practice these days,' I replied.

'There's a tennis court at our Dacha.' Kate answered proudly.

'And a Banya,' Galina laughed, 'where we hit you with birch twigs.'

The next day we drove some fifty miles outside the city into barren, flat countryside stopping only once at an indoor food market, an enormous warehouse, the largest market I had ever seen under one roof. Food from every part of Russia was on display. Nowhere had I seen such a variety of fish, meat, alcohol, stalls of venison, pheasant and duck, flowers and vegetables all under one roof. Fishmongers were selling roe and caviar straight from the Volga, Caspian and Lake Baikal. At a large tank, filled with live Cray fish, Sasha bought enough for all us to indulge that weekend.

A silent, narrow road, to their Dacha, was pock marked and at times merely a wide dirt track that raised clouds of dust. We rolled through unattended farm land stretching forever each side of the road. In the distance I could see the boundless flat landscape of the Steppes. Not one person anywhere in sight, nor horses, which surprised me because I thought Russia was a land of horses, no pigs, no sheep or fowl and certainly no birds winging across the clear and empty sky. I tried to imagine the great Cossack leader, Stenka Razin, galloping over this wild scenery, calling to his feared, and free, horsemen brotherhood, 'Zaporozhskii, Yaik,' and seeing them, once more, join together in their unruly cavalry storm.

'Tell me,' I asked Sasha, 'Was it better under Stalin do you think?'

'Certainly,' Sasha replied emphatically.

'In what way?' I asked dubiously curious since Stalin, according to historians, had been responsible for fifteen to twenty million people dying across Russia and the Ukraine from starvation, Gulag interment and random terror purges.

'We all had the things we needed, good education, a home for everyone, and work.'

'What about all the people that died under Stalin?'

'I don't know about that, they didn't die around here. Samara is the power house of Russia. If you worked hard, tried your best, there were always good opportunities for everyone, no matter who you or your family were.'

Sasha had been born during Stalin's dictatorship and worked hard for the Communist Party. Successful he became a local politician. He wasn't the only Russian I was to meet who believed life in Soviet Russia was far better than in 'New Russia'.

Kate was interpreting, Galina nodding in agreement.

'In Britain you give us bad press,' Sasha said, 'But you know it wasn't us who dropped an atomic bomb, on Japanese civilians, and it wasn't us who dropped toxic Agent Orange on villagers it was Americans who did that. You should be giving them a bad press.' He addressed me, without anger, bluntly stating a common Russian opinion.

I hadn't thought of any of these things and had no reply.

'It is why you should be more afraid of America than Russia,' young Kate added. 'The West also blames us for Chechnya but it isn't true. Chechens are murderous criminals and Islamic terrorists.'

Along a narrow dirt road we came to a large, two storey, wooden Dacha reminding me of the country houses of Imperial Russia's estate owners.

'I designed it myself,' Sasha said proudly staring at it.

Inside were rooms of lofty ceilings and outside, apple and plum orchards hung languidly in the afternoon heat, heavy with fruit. Scattered between the trees were vegetable gardens filled with carrot, cabbage and onion.

Across the dirt road, in front of his Dacha, Sasha proudly showed me their private tennis court. Gazing down the country road, devoid of any trees or shrubs, I could see another large Dacha, with a sleek thoroughbred grazing in a field. The only horse I had seen that day.

Galina and Olga, vociferously laughing, happy to be there, prepared food in their wide kitchen, filled with wooden tables and benches, cooking cray fish, chicken and salad which they then carried outside to a ten feet long pine table.

After lunch and wine we sat chatting in the sultry afternoon sunshine.

Russians love open air dining, a centuries old tradition, of family gatherings. During summer's hot months families desert cities to go to Dacha and country retreats. There's no better description of it than in Chekov's, 'Cherry Orchard'.

'Let's cycle,' Sasha suggested.

Four push bikes were wheeled out.

'Momma will show you some woods and a lake where you can swim,' Kate enthused.

It was a hot, cloudless day with temperatures in the eighties.

'We're going to visit friends,' Kate said.

Galina changed into cycling shorts and blouse, I removed my shirt and off we pedalled into the wild landscape.

Cycling along dirt path we came to a silent Tsarist village of carved wooden houses, remnants of a once thriving old hamlet. The design of these wooden Izbas had remained unchanged since the days of Peter the Great. In Imperial Russia they would have been painted brightly, detailed with motifs of animals, birds, flowers and tracery, wooden lace and crosses adorning them, carved and brightly coloured. The carvings were still there and the sloping, shingle wood, tent roofs but the joyful, artistic colours had faded away.

Village cottages were built to withstand the extremes of a Russian climate of minus 20c winters followed by sweltering, dry summers. Wood was ideal for such rigors and Russia a land of great forests. Peasants built their homes one storey, rich merchants and gentry two.

If one compares Log Cabins of the American frontier with these Russian dwellings, built in the same period, the difference between a western love of utility and the creative, romantic mind of the Slav is undeniably apparent.

I had rarely seen such a timeless setting. Here in this rustic village of wood I could easily imagine bearded Russians, in colourful kaftans, socialising in the street, troikas appearing on frosty forest roads, children in furs playing in the snow.

Richard Chancellor, visiting Russia in the 16th century, wrote of them, "The common houses of the country are everywhere built of beams of fir," then went on to describe them as being four square, resisting the cold and expelling all winds that blow. It was the kind of place Turgenev wrote of in his delightful 'Hunters Sketches.' The confined dirt road, we cycled over, ran between these

The Volga River, Samara.

Volga Embankment, Samara.

Tsarist Building, Samara.

Tsarist Dwelling, Samara.

28

Tsarist Prison, Samara. Now a medical student Hall of Residence.

Babushka on street of pre-revolution wood buildings.

Old Samara, street of wood dwellings.

Drama Theatre, Samara.

timeless wooden dwellings, now owned by New Russians, city businessmen and mafia, using them as weekend summer retreats.

Cycling beyond the village we came to an unfinished concrete road. It was such a dry, hot day. I tied my shirt across my shoulders for protection against the sun. We cycled into dense, deciduous woodland of birch and larch on a track so restricted and filled with potholes we had to get off our bikes and walk. This wild-wood was so claustrophobically overgrown, the path barely discernible, I realised how easy it would be to get lost in these great forests of Russia. In a journal I once read how in northern Russian forests a group of 'Old Believers' had been discovered who were unaware of the demise of Tsarist Russia, the Revolution or of New Russia. At first I had disbelieved this story, as a Russian urban myth, but then one day saw a photograph of a wooden mansion, the former home of a Tsarist landowner, lying empty in the middle of a birch forest. Trees had grown all round it, and through it, when its owners had long disappeared. Until recently no one had known it was there.

'Where are we going?' I asked.

'To a lake were we can swim,' Galina smiled.

Russians love wild swimming, they do it in every lake, stream and river, just as Sasha had done in the Volga. After one struggling hour we reached an isolated lake, several hundred yards across, which I thought too brackish to swim in. Its calm isolation amid towering, glowering trees and its silence gave the place an air of ominous anger. There were no sounds of life nor were there fowl on this hidden lake.

Galina removed her shorts and cotton blouse, under which she wore a bikini, and dived in. I sat on the bank watching, thinking the whole scene like something out of a fairy tale. If a goblin or ogre had suddenly appeared at that moment out of the silver birches it would have been what I expected. On many occasions in Russia I experienced this other reality sensation, not so much a walking back in time as a stepping into some chimerical phantasy. It happened in old monasteries, palaces, parks and tsarist villages that somehow seemed to exist in a realm beyond the edge of time.

Galina called, 'Come in.'

'I don't have swimming trunks.'

'In Russia we don't care about this.' She laughed, playfully bemused at such reticence.

In a short while, without any self–consciousness, Galina lifted herself from the cold water of the lake,   removed her bikini and, completely naked, dried off
with a towel she had tucked in her bike saddlebag. She wasn't going to let such an inconsequential thing spoil her pleasure of sun and exercise.

Later I asked her, 'Weren't you afraid I might try to take advantage of you?'

Galina pushed me playfully. Laughing she said. 'Of course not, you're an Englishman.'

Russians, used to living in large family units of cousins and distant relatives, that frequently meet, or drop by for a visit, have none of the reserve about naked bodies that we have in the west.   During the Soviet period, and still to a large extent today, most Russians lived in large, communal flats sharing bathrooms and kitchens that hardly included privacy.

We had cycled far and perhaps due to the oppressive heat of the day and wild swimming, Galina had lost all sense of direction or recall of which road we should take home. On the Russian Steppes this could have been fatal. We had no mobile phone with us. The sun had fallen and beginning to turn the horizon golden red.

From years of wandering lonely places I had made a mental note of the sun's position before we set out on our journey. This simple procedure had often guided me home when lost in forests, deserts and even cities and on this occasion navigated us safely back to the dacha.

After a light meal, in late evening, Sasha stoked the Banya. We sat in clouds of steam, towels round our waists, occasionally plunging ourselves beneath a cold shower. We beat each other humorously, with twigs, to make our bodies tingle before returning to sweat on steamy benches.

Katya didn't join us but occasionally peaked through chinks in the door, prudishly fretting, in youthful disgust at the whole procedure. Afterwards we drank wine and vodka and ate sweet cakes made especially by Olga and Katya.

The Dacha bedroom allotted me was the largest I have ever slept in, like a conference room, with a bed in the middle. Its wooden floors were covered by brightly coloured rugs, its windows were shuttered on all sides and chandeliers filled the room with light. The bed was big enough for a family of giants.

Morning came brightly. Opening the window I could smell the fields and see across the vast flat vista of the Russian Steppes.

That day we played tennis. Russians are more sports minded than any nation I ever came across including Americans and it is rare to meet any Russian who has never been part of an athletic team of some kind. Sasha and Olga both had been champion tennis players, Galina an accomplished swimmer. At Rhodes I had seen her swim far out into the Mediterranean Sea and sport in it like a dolphin. Since the fall of Communism Russians have continued this love of sport and now add to it a healthier lifestyle based on

Hollywood images of beauty copied from American films. Women city dwellers attend gyms regularly, adhere to strict diets and socially wear, unselfconsciously, the most revealing of dresses.

That weekend Sasha and I worked in the gardens of the Dacha, digging post holes for new fencing and reinforcing others. Sasha spoke no English but was a kindly companion as he gesticulated his directions. Afterwards we sat outside, in the fading glow of the sun, drinking Georgian wine before visiting Sasha's neighbour at the nearby property fifty yards further down the road. This recently constructed Dacha was even more splendid and larger than Sasha's.

'This is Sergei.' Galina introduced.

Sergei was six feet, bare chested, athletically built. Galina affectionately, admiringly, touched his biceps as she introduced us. Kate gave her mother a reproving glance.

Sasha seemed reluctant to speak much with Sergei, there was a distrusting resentment there I thought, but Galina would have talked to him all night. He was another prosperous New Russian whose business no one discussed. I looked around trying to discover what this man, of about thirty years, did for a living. He was indeed affluent, the size of his two storeys Dacha attested to it, but I found no clues. When I asked Galina what he did she gave the answer I was to hear all over Russia whenever I asked such a question.

'He is in business,' she replied.

'What sort of business?' I probed.

'Oh, he buys and sells things.'

That I was to learn, with time, was often the Russian answer. Russians keep secrets better than anyone. It indicated Sergei's business was questionable and was perhaps why Sasha avoided him.

'Tomorrow we go home.' Kate said sadly. She loved being with her grandparents.

'And the day after I'll take you to Tolyatti,' Sasha smiled.

'Far?

'From Samara 80 kilometres,' Galina commented.

Back at Galina's, the following morning, after breakfast, I strolled down the immaculately tidy grassy hill, of the residential complex, admiring its grand view over the Volga, then walked to Volsky Prospect.

Beside the Volga embankment, a wide, road leads past a gigantic beer factory, the best known in all of Russia, the home of Zhiguli Beer filling the air with its intoxicating aroma.

The day was hot, the sky a dusty pale violet. On the long Volsky road the only other pedestrian, an old woman shabbily dressed, seemed to be struggling against life itself.

Zhiguli Brewery, surrounded by an enormous wall, that gives it the appearance of a Soviet prison, was opened in 1881 by an Austrian with the magnificent, never ending, name of Alfred Josef Marie Ritter von Vakano, during those Tsarist Imperial days when Germans and Austrians were welcome in Russia before the time they were seen as bourgeoisie enemies.

Zhiguli beer can reach levels of fifteen percent alcohol and the bottles have enticing names, Von Vakano Dark, Von Vakano Light or more simply Samara Beer, which all Russians boast is the best beer in the world.

Beyond, and rising above the forbidding walls, are enormous brewery towers clumped together like organ pipes. The heady odor, surrounding the factory, welcomes you closer like some long lost friend or treacherous enemy. At the end of the long brewery wall you arrive at, three storeyed, wrought iron balconied, buildings entranced by impressive iron gates.

Adjoining the brewery is a dilapidated building, of a military headquarters, with armed soldiers guarding its entrance. Next to these headquarters, in the brewery wall is a faucet, at which locals come to fill glass and plastic bottles, of any size, with their favourite beer. To do this the brewery charges a miniscule fee. I watched intrigued as men and women filled their three and five litre plastic bottles, with beer from the tap, under the attentive eyes of two soldiers guarding the military complex. Only in Russia would anyone put an army headquarters next to a beer factory. The beer at the faucet was so extremely cheap even the most penurious could afford it and it seemed as though Russia encouraged alcoholism. In time I discovered Russia did nothing to combat drug abuse either.

Zhiguli beer is genuinely excellent and because it comes in a range of alcoholic strengths it is possible to enjoy it according to one's mood and tolerance or the occasion. It has never to my knowledge become popular in the West no doubt due protectionism and its inexpensive superiority.

Before Soviet industrialisation, the Volga, having its birth in a pristine icy north was chemical free and so unpolluted that the Volga was an ideal choice of place to open a brewery. Then, during Soviet times, Mother Volga, the Queen of all rivers, became toxically innocuous from chemical works, refineries and industries, that made Samara the power house of Russia but it was no longer good for making beer or for Russian genetics. This pollution however didn't stop Zhiguli Brewery which continued to help, or poison, struggling Russians drown the pain of war, poverty, hunger and oppression that now began to stalk Russia's struggling humanity. The pendulum of time always swings to its opposite side and now, in Capitalist Russia, this loveliest of rivers is once more clean and clear and Zhiguli beer once more highly prized.

Past the Zhiguli I noticed roads were being widened, obviously to expand capability of the nearby army complex. At the end of the tiring road I came to a corner café booth. Galina had caught up with me and we spoke briefly.

'I want to visit my mother, alone, just for a few minutes to see how she is. Perhaps you can have   coffee here while I am away?' She suggested, apologetically.

In the morning sun, I sat outside, at a weathered metal table, drinking awful coffee, wishing I had helped myself at the Zhiguli faucet. The café was just an open air booth, on a small corner strip of land, in front of which were an accommodating half dozen tables. The woman serving me smiled delighted to see a foreigner. After a quiet moment my thoughts and peace were interrupted by a drunken Russian youth, in his twenties, whose feet, like his sandy hair, were all over the place. Mumbling to me, incoherently gesturing and looking as though he were about to fall to the pavement, he wasn't threatening. I got up, leaving my half-finished coffee on the table, and walked away, unable to understand his words, or waving arms, leaving him still shouting after me.

Whenever alone in Samara something like this happened to me. Russian drunks find foreigners easy game, and instinctively recognising them, they approach smiling. I tried to avoid them whenever I saw them. I never heard of them murdering or assaulting anyone, which is done usually only by organised gangs, but they are nevertheless a nuisance. Never trying to rob or be aggressive they just wanted to talk to a foreigner.

Samara is a delight, everywhere enormous trees, wide roads, well maintained parks, yet for all its expansive, artistic and cultured appearance, it seemed to bestow a sad loneliness on everyone walking its streets. I watched a troubled scatter of humanity, opulent, poor, aged visiting country folk, office workers and businessmen passing me along silent roads. They always appeared to be wandering, lost in confusion, through a vast empty landscape as though seeking redemption for themselves.

I decided to walk more of these sparse streets and hopefully meet up with Galina later.

Samara has preserved many of its wooden houses. In the outer suburbs these structures are one storey and raised on stilts. One I came across was leaning precariously, a supporting stilt had either rotted away or been sawn in half by a malicious neighbour. I photographed it and left hurriedly to avoid a passing Russian who had paused to stare at me as though he were about to cross the road and confront me.

Close to the inner city are some magnificent two storey wooden houses that had once belonged to Samara's wealthy merchants prior to Revolution. They were grand and captured my attention. Galina hadn't mentioned these. Discovering them for myself was a delight. Walking down a dirt path, between them, I noticed they were not the single houses I had at first supposed but were several wooden dwellings joined to form a central court. Wooden steps, with carved banisters, led to upper floors. On peaceful streets outside, heavy-weight grandmas, (Babushkas), sat on wicker chairs sunning themselves and I wished my Russian had been fluent enough to converse with them, listen to their tales of old Samara and their own troubled childhoods. The world changes rapidly and one day their memories, of lost times and things known, will be gone forever.

I wandered back to the corner café booth to look for Galina. The young drunk was still there and this time he came, in a friendly, inoffensive way, to tell me something again which I couldn't understand. Later I realised he was trying to tell me Galina had returned and was trying to find me. Wherever I travelled in Russia there were young inebriated males, drowning their despair in alcohol and drugs, attempting to escape the debilitating hopelessness of their lives. Impolitely I walked away, following the road home, past the lengthy prison like wall and inviting smell of the Zhiguli Beer factory. Then some intuition urged me to turn back to return to the café. Half way there I saw the unmistakable, femininely elegant, Galina hurrying towards me.

Galina, throwing her arms around me, admonished 'I was so worried about you. It's dangerous for foreigners alone in Samara.'

Russians generally believe foreigners are attacked on their streets. I never was, but found this protective concern for visitors an insight into the mind and heart of the Russian people.

At about ten the following morning Sasha, Olga, Galina and the authoritative teen Kate arrived to take me to Tolyatti. I sat in the rear between Galina and Kate. Following the great bend of the Volga, the road heading west, Sasha stopped frequently to visit businesses. Although I tried to understand what his purpose was in doing it, he made no comment nor did Galina or Kate, he just went inside to talk privately but never purchased items.

Mother Volga, serenely wide and peaceful, flowed quietly, taking time on her long journey. On the distant side of the river I could see the rising hills of the Zhigulis. Here the bend of the Volga, formed by an ancient shift in tectonic plates, doubles back on itself in a gigantic arc that almost turns the expanse of the Zhiguli Mountains into an island. To call the Zhiguli's mountains is a bit of a misnomer, the highest peak is only 371 metres, but on the vast, flat Russian landscape they make a spectacular and unusual sight. Russian guide books refer to them as 'The Pearl of Russia' and with the wonder of the mighty Volga, on three sides, giving grand views from its hills of the interminable gridiron expanse of forest and plain, one can understand why.

Catching my mood and silence Galina remarked, 'My friend Tanya is hoping to take us there one day soon,'

'One of our famous artists, Ilya Repin, lived there. Have you heard of him?' Kate quizzed as she pointed at the hills.

'Yes,' I whispered.

'Oh! I didn't know he lived there,' Galina said in surprise.

Sasha, who loved his granddaughter, smiled in approval.

Repin is most famously known for his painting, 'Hauliers on The Volga' in which a weary, harnessed team of exhausted serfs, tow an enormous, heavy barge along the Volga River. Repin had painted this scene from life and had known the eleven men personally. More than anything this painting exposed the abject, painful, miserable reality of life of 19th century Russians. Repin's art is always emotional, larger than life. His images of Cossacks are quite incredible and all his art is filled with boundless energy, detail, and dazzling colour.

Galina remarked, 'Zhiguli is a very beautiful place filled with deep gorges, caves and cliffs.'

After one hour Sasha pulled off the road. We stopped beside a two storey structure that looked like an oversized barn. Climbing a flight of wooden steps we entered a room resembling a workman's hut which, during Soviet times, it probably had been. Long, wooden trestle, tables with benches filled its central space. Beyond them a kitchen served food from a robust wooden counter top.

We ate beef and vegetable dinners. Conscious of their appearance, as all New Russian women are, Kate and Galina ate only half their dinner and refused desert.

Back on the road a forest of deciduous trees, hanging melancholy, hid everything. After miles along a bad road, to our right, was a huge complex of wooden chalets, and holiday homes, set among neat lawns and mature trees

'That would be a nice place for me to stay sometime,' I commented.

Sasha shook his head in warning, 'No not there.' He scowled at the place as he turned his gaze back to the road. He didn't elaborate, Galina remained silent. I knew not to pursue the matter but later found out it is one of the favourite, fraternising, resorts of Tolyatti's notorious gangster elite.

Turning onto a side road that led beside the Volga we entered a large park. We were the only people there. Sasha stopped at a vast expanse of water, the Samara Reservoir which is the third largest man-made lake in the world, 22 miles wide and 310 miles long, with a shore line of 1618 miles and so huge it is often called the Samara Sea. There are ten towns along its verdant banks. Three towns have disappeared, from the former Volga River embankment, to be rebuilt above the waterline of this enormous reservoir.

Overlooking the lake is an impressive, pedestalled, monument of a bronze horseman, a towering statue of Vasili Tatishchev, the 18th Century founder of the cities of Stavropol on Volga, Perm and Ekaterinburg, a man of immense, tireless talent, architect, soldier, statesman, economist, ethnographer, and author of the first five volume comprehensive history of Russia and a dictionary of the Russian language. Tatishchev had risen to prominence under

Peter the Great. His once beautiful, famous, city of Stavropol on Volga, over which this reservoir has been built, was flooded, with its lovely Church and old mansions, in Soviet times, and now all lie forgotten beneath the vast lake. Instead of a magnificent Tsarist town we now have the new city of Tolyatti further along the Volga.

Not a breath of wind stalked across the lake. No birds dappled the sunlight of its waters, everywhere whispered a disconcerting despondency. Hundreds of years of laughing and living have been interred beneath this man-made enormous reservoir. The statue of Tatishchev seems to be pointing a raised arm and accusing finger, at the destruction of his lost city, gone forever.

The 46 feet high pedestal, on which the statue stands, is of limestone quarried from the Zhiguli Mountains, which are visible across the colossal lake. Impressive, but I was haunted by the loneliness of it all, no sightseers, or lovers, or people with dogs. Often I have experienced this desolate loneliness, beside man made dams and lakes, as if nature itself, angry at this intrusion is patiently, waiting for revenge.

I took a photo, beneath the monument, of Olga, Kate and Galina idling and leaning on Sasha, who stood between them like a Russian bear, with his family clutching him for comfort and protection.

We drove on to Tolyatti. This most depressing looking city imaginable was built to replace Stavropol on Volga. Tolyatti city exudes regimented, soulless uniformity and bleak utility of a violent Communist era. Towering high-rise flats, without any creativity to lessen their dejected, monotonous facades, were everywhere. We drove through wide, forlorn streets that looked as though built for tank warfare or rapid movement of troops. On each side, of a laser straight main street, were shops, mostly empty of customers. To walk to them, across such a wide expanse of road, probably discouraged shopping anyway, I thought. Without a vehicle, in this city of vehicles, life would be a struggle. The appalling Soviet style buildings, unhappily copied by British Labour Party architects in the 1950s and 60s are, just as in Britain, given over to graffiti, poverty and violence. Not surprisingly Tolyatti became a place of mafia gangsters and government corruption.

Similarities between Tolyatti and America's Chicago are ironic. Tolyatti, a city of car manufacture and mafia gangsters, was named after, Palmiro Togliatti, who had been leader of the Italian Communist Party for forty years. A puppet of Stalin, Kruschev and Brezhnev Togliatti had been responsible for developing Russia's, AutoVaz, automobile plant in partnership with Italy's Fiat motor cars.

Palmiro Togliatti was targeted three times, and shot at in assassination attempts, but like his close friends Mao Tse-tung and Stalin, he was a survivor and didn't die. These untouchable friends, Mao, Stalin and Togliatti attended Stalin's last, lavish birthday Party in 1948.

No one could have invented such a tale, a city of automobiles, created by an Italian, built by a Soviet regime that opposed almost everything American yet adopting all the violence of the Italian mafia plagued American automobile city.

There have been, approximately 100 contract killings per year in Tolyatti, mostly connected to control of Russia's car industry that is partnered, not only with Fiat but also with America's General Motors. Not all these killings are however business related, five journalists were assassinated, three architects attacked and one killed and the head of local administration, Anatoly Stepanov, murdered. One city mayor Nikolay Utkin was jailed for seven years for extortion and corruption. A journalist Valery Ivanov was shot three times in the head and four times in the chest as he left his apartment. It was generally believed this contract killing had been ordered by the city's mayor Sergey Zhilkin, who was himself later assassinated.

That's one side of Tolyatti but if you turn a blind eye to all the corruption, and murders, the place has some of the finest sporting facilities in the whole of Russia. This city was intended to be an example of Soviet excellence and the perfect Soviet person, which simply meant physical perfection. Every kind of sport is represented here. Some of Russia's top athletes have made Tolyatti their home because of its unparalleled facilities.

Numerous international companies have also found it lucrative to be in Tolyatti, ship building, the largest ammonia manufacturing plant in Russia, electronics industries, petrochemicals and many others

Tolyatti is also a venue for one of the largest international folk festivals in the world, attracting more than 130,000 visitors each July and has grown so large it is compelled to use two sites in the Zhiguli Mountains. Singers from every corner of the world gather, from Canada, UK, New Zealand, USA, Japan, Israel, to mention just a few. Not surprisingly Israel since nearby Samara has built the largest Synagogue in the whole of Russia and one of the largest in the world.

On our journey out of Tolyatti Sasha seemed noticeably anxious. Several times Galina asked if he would stop at an apteka, (chemist), but he didn't seem to hear. We passed numerous aptekas but he made no attempt to stop until on the outskirts of the city. Sasha had been a Tolyatti politician and worked in the automotive industry. It was obvious he wanted to get out of this dangerous place – "When evil reigns the people hide".

On a quiet part of the road, half way to Samara City, two policemen with that fabricated, sternness police put on with their uniforms each day, were standing on a stretch of highway where dense woods flanked the road. They waved us to stop. Sasha drove past, for about fifty yards, out of hearing distance, stopped and walked back to the waiting police. Watching from the rear window I saw him reach inside his coat for his internal passport then open his wallet and he gave them something but I couldn't see what. A policeman nodded politely to him. My guess was he had given them money but I couldn't be certain. Returning to the vehicle Sasha's face gave nothing away and none of us asked what had happened.

Over time I learned no matter what Russian Police charged you with, or robbed you of, they always did it with expressionless faces. Your safest strategy was to do the same.

Although my Russian language was inadequate I decided it was imperative to explore alone. A chance came when Galina returned to employment at a small private bank. I made my way up the steep, tree scattered slope of the Volga embankment and on to Samara City. It was a calm, bright, beautiful day.

Samara's streets are spotlessly clean and by European standards uncrowded. In the city centre I came to a long street filled with marketeers selling mostly clothes. At the head of the street, where the market began, stood a tall, athletic, cold faced man in his late twenties observing all that happened. His appearance was military but there was no uniform. He was one of the, protection racketeering, thugs that haunt markets, businesses and all Russian cities.

Sitting huddled like a pile of unwashed garments, a totally forlorn old lady sat on the pavement beside a woven basket. Her clothes shabby she looked emaciated. I dropped a US. dollar in her basket. Dollars are preferred currency in Russia, considered more stable than the rouble. Hand trembling, her crumpled face gave me the most surprised glance at such a large sum in her meagre kopek collection of coins. Over my shoulder I noticed the street thug or guard, whatever he was, watching us also in surprise.

Not all the street market traders were Russian. There was an Italian, handsome, youthful, selling tee shirts and selling more than anyone else due to his looks. Russian women, passionate about Italian men, just stopped to throng his stall while perusing his range of shirts.

Beyond this street market I came to a road dominated by fashionable shops and cafes and out of curiosity entered a shop selling antiques and militaria. An array of swords from Russia and Europe, some hundreds of years old, were on display. Behind a glass counter were bejewelled icons. The cabinets filled with jewellery, porcelain, silver drinking vessels and daggers from Tsarist Russia, astounded me. Nowhere in England or Europe had I seen such an Aladdin's treasure as this.

The owner of the store, young, flamboyantly smart, fashionably elegant, wearing gold chain and amulet, coloured shirt and soft leather shoes, spoke excellent English as he showed me various icons.

'I don't think I am allowed to take Russian antiques out of the country,' I reminded him.

'There are ways to do this. I can give you a document approving the sale. It allows you to take them with you.'

I didn't buy anything because taking anything out of Russia, more than 50 years old, is subject to very strict laws and anything over 100 years forbidden entirely. Though icons cannot be taken out of Russia they are sometimes smuggled through the Ukraine and into the wider world. Frequently the ones on sale in Russia are fakes from Turkey, or have been stolen. Russian ruling regarding non export applies to all antiques but even when you comply with all the required paperwork, of sellers export certificates and receipts, you can still find at Russian Customs some official will confiscate your purchase, supposedly for verification. You will be told you can pick it up on your next visit to Russia and you never see it again.

Leaving this exclusive shopping area I wandered into another broad square of more amenable market vendors. Galina had told me she loved yellow roses. I'd remembered because of the charming way she had said, 'Yallo Rozes,' in her distinctly Russian accent so I decided to buy her a yellow rose bouquet.

This large open air market offered a wide choice of goods, Russian hats, fur coats, general produce, fish, vegetables, fruit and facing me across the square a long line of florists with creative displays. A scent of flowers, drifting over the market transformed the broken tarmac and empty morning.

Approaching a florist, who recognised I was foreign even before I spoke, asked too much for her roses so I moved on to another flower seller who quoted the same price. I was sure she had heard my conversation, further down the line, but the bouquet she offered was truly magnificent so bought it.

Russian florists create the most dazzling bouquets. Wherever one travels, in this enormous country, flowers are displayed in markets, on city streets and corner booths, rescuing life, love and beauty, from the toils of rush and commerce.

It was a hot, long day; the walk back to Volzhsky Prospect unfavourable to preserving the bouquet of flowers I now held, hanging downwards, in my right hand. Near the market I noticed buses. Going over to find one home I asked a tall Russian woman for direction. When I asked for a bus to Volski Prospect she, laughing at my English, said numbers in Russian that I couldn't understand. Making a gesture of counting with my fingers she was delighted but still couldn't help. Shrugging my shoulders I began the six mile trek back to the Volga. A light breeze sprang up, rippling the wide expanse of river, dissipating the sultry heat of the afternoon. Samara's streets were quiet, and views across the Volga majestic.

Russia's infinite emptiness is felt everywhere, even in large cities and here is still room to pause, admire and reflect in this broad country. At work Russians are among the most indefatigable people on earth yet always display an aura of stillness about them I believe absorbed from this vast land.

Back home I put the flowers in water and set off to meet Galina, at the small bank she worked in. It was another three mile walk but the evening a delight.

Arriving early I waited outside the bank. Just down the road were two men, watching, from a dilapidated car. Their appearance of suspicious scrutiny I had learned to associate with police and military.

The bank, in which Galina worked, had locked security door. No one could enter without ringing a buzzer. I made no attempt to enter just walked up and down outside. The doors of the bank suddenly opened, and closed firmly, to confront me with two burly men, staring aggressively and calling me over.

'What are you doing here?' I was asked in Russian.

'Waiting for Mrs Kosireva,.' I stared back adding, 'I am English,'

'Ah!' came back a satisfied grunt as the men returned inside and secured the door.

48

There are many small banks in Russia specifically created to launder money and hide criminal transactions. Putin is doing his best to close these and force criminals to use established larger, more reputable, banks where questionable activities can be more accurately monitored. Galina told me Sasha found her work at this one and she was sure the government would close it down soon.

Corruption is everywhere in Russia and evident almost daily. Surprisingly homicide is less than in the USA and although Russian Police claim most homicides are alcohol related but statistics show that much of it is due to mafia gangs of the oligarchs. Adding to this omnipresent corruption is collusion with Russian police.

Galina, wide eyed at the flowers and the fact I had walked six miles with them, smiled happily at the yellow roses and after smelling them several times twirled around the room in delight before placing them in a vase. We drank a glass of wine, and ate a little, waiting for Katya to come home from her grandparents so I could take them to dinner. After a shower Galina returned to the living room, dressed in black skirt and white blouse, to insert a CD in her music console. The music was from the film 'Grease'. She was laughing, happily, quietly to herself and I expected her to come and sit beside me, instead she stood directly in front of me waiting for the song, 'You're the One that I Want,' to come on and then began singing.

'You the Wolla Walont, Ooh, Ooh, Ooh.'

I laughed at her. Russian women are prone to moments of madness. She ignored me and began a dancing striptease to the music her arms swaying above her head like tree branches in a storm and hips swinging like some exotic pendula until her skirt fell to her feet. She flung off her blouse, then her clothes were removed down to panties and bra and, just as suddenly as she had begun, she stopped and sat down beside me. We sat together laughing. Galina didn't understand the words of the song completely. I didn't try to correct her since I had never understood Travolta's words either. It was after all just Galina's humorous, unselfconscious, Russian way of saying thank you for the flowers.

Katya came home and we all went to dinner.

For decades, during the Communist period and latter part of Tsarist rule, Russians shared apartments, dissected into tiny bed sitters, with shared facilities. Centuries before this period they lived communally in isolated villages and so they are consequentially, innately uninhibited. That doesn't however mean promiscuous, Russian women often exhibit an indignant prudery to any kind of unwanted sexual approach, especially younger women born after the collapse of the iron curtain. They carry an unapproachable personal dignity, pride and sense of decorum lacking in the West. Russians generally are welcoming, highly sociable and able to be themselves, without pretence in any company, revelling in family gatherings, weekend celebrations and parties.

The following day I went to explore, alone again, while Kate stayed with her grandparents and Galina worked. It was a cool morning of grey skies as I strolled the long Volga Embankment and Promenade. Samara's Promenade has been described as one of the longest and most beautiful Promenades in the world and I believe it.

Beside the Volga, through lovely gardens, I walked admiring the abundance of flowers and lofty trees. Who tells you of these places in Western commentaries? Vegetation flourishes here as nowhere else due to loamy, acidic soil. Russia's trees are taller and broader than anywhere I have visited in Europe. The height of the ubiquitous Russian birches makes our English ones seem dwarfish in comparison. Maples, common all over the northern hemisphere, flourish best in Russia and nowhere else can you find poplars like Russia's towering, gigantic cottonwoods.

On this delightful walk again I noticed a lack of bird or animal life and just as I had in Tatishev Park, near Tolyatti. There was no bird song and only a squirrel could be seen sometimes but nothing else. I recalled I hadn't seen foxes in the evenings on the great swathes of lawns and green spaces that separated the blocks of flats where Galina lived and I speculated whether there could be some kind of pollution, emanating from the varied, numerous, chemical industries Samara is renowned for, just as there had been in Stalin's days. This passing reverie didn't distract me long beside the unforgettable enchantment of the wide, wonderful Volga.

The oldest recorded name for the stupendous Volga appropriately means 'Mystical Stream', and whenever I was near it I thought it the only place I would gladly live beside forever. Walking toward a quay, where Volga cruise ships moor on a 1800 mile journey to the Caspian Sea, I noticed a man, in a dark suit, leaning with his hands on the promenade embankment wall, gazing over the expansive, captivating river. Immediately I realised he was British. How I knew I don't know, something about his body language, or ease of manner perhaps, but something decidedly British. I walked over to him and asked, 'Do you speak English?'

Turning to me grinning he said, 'Yes, I'm English, from London.'

After introducing myself I asked, 'Are you on holiday? You know you are the first Englishman, in fact the first foreigner I've met since I arriving here,' I continued.

'I'm a salesman with a British lubricant company'. He held out his hand. 'There's a lot of engineering here and actually there are a lot of foreigners but they fly in and out and don't stay long.'

'Until recently I had no idea this place existed. None of the guide books mentioned it much,' I said.

'There are many wonderful cities in Russia not just this one. You know what surprises me, the number of women and so few men.' He looked out over the Volga deep in thought. 'They say it's because so many Russian men died in the war.'

'That was some time ago and doesn't really explain it now.' I suggested.

'Some cities are worse than this one. Rostov-na-Donu for instance has three times more women than men and you have to admit the women here are more beautiful than anywhere else on earth'

It was a sultry day, the Volga unhurriedly flowing with barely a ripple. A cargo vessel passed in the distance. After comparing our impressions of Russia for a while we shook hands and said, 'Goodbye.'

Reflecting, on the man's comments, I wondered whether there was a connection between scarcity of animal life and shortage of men in Russia. There is a sequel to this conversation because later, after concluding my Russian odyssey, back in London at a hotel bar I broke into conversation about Russia with a man sitting next to me. I mentioned this disparity between the numbers of men and women in Russia.

'Ah! Well there is a reason for that. I'm a geneticist with an oil company. We know something happened to the male chromosome in Russia.' He told me in a matter of fact way. 'So far we don't know what caused it specifically, but we are certain it occurred.'

Intrigued by his comment, and after a little research, I found an article that explained fertility rates had been falling in Russia for decades, due to the industrial pollutants of the Soviet period, but it had only become apparent to Russian scientists in the 1980s -90s. Unfortunately the problem continues still. Most studies assert it is due to the prevalence of alcoholism, and smoking among men, as well as long term environmental damage. Statistics show however that alcoholism and smoking are in decline in Russia so we are left with the hypothesis of pollution. At the moment it is believed contaminated industrial run-offs, into rivers and lakes, has affected the natural habitat and health of the Russian people. By the 1990s Russia had one of the highest death rates, outside wartime, in all of Europe.

These explanations still didn't satisfy my curiosity because from my own observation I noticed it wasn't a lack of fertility in families I had met in Russia but quite simply far more girls were being born than boys.

Beside me moored on the Volga were, four tiered, 120 cabin, cruise ships. The quay was quiet and the cruisers empty. All passengers must have disembarked on one of their daily tours. On the quay a few, weary looking, souvenir sellers were displaying inexpensive mementos. On a trellis table my eyes caught a series of six fold-out maps that charted the whole 2000 miles long Volga River. I bought them and, back in the Volzhsky apartment, spread them out on a carpet to see the whole length of the Volga. The maps stretched fourteen feet in length.

Volga cruising has a long history, Alexander Dumas, the French novelist, came to Samara on a cruise to Astrakhan. With French refinement he was so dismayed at the depth of the Volga mud on Samara's river banks he didn't visit the city at all, which is a great pity for the rest of us.

Once, near the place I stood, there had been a most magnificent Cathedral, the Voskresenski Sobor, that had delighted ferry and ship passengers so much they came to the decks just to see it. It has gone now because it wasn't quite what Stalin wanted, a work of art that celebrated religion, in his atheist state system. Soviets, in the dark, night after night, blew it up. Russia had always been known as 'Holy Russia' so devout Samarans began secretly collecting broken fragments of their beloved Cathedral.

After the Cathedral had disappeared into dusty rubble and broken death Bolsheviks stole the Cathedral's treasures and old icons. Stalin had his own war-time bunker built, one hundred and twenty feet, beneath where the Cathedral had been, an act among many of his, of deliberate evil. He had entered the womb of this once magnificent Cathedral to say to everyone, 'Communism is now our God and I am its Saviour'.

Samarans however never forgot their lovely Cathedral and since the fall of Communism a new one has been built.

You would think when political systems, religious hierarchies and others begin destroying works of art and libraries, and start murdering people who disagree with them, that after thousands of years of this kind of vandalism and destruction, a lesson would have been learned that such regimes are evil, limited by time and the conscience of man.

My walk led me on to the broad, untidy, space of Chapaev Square. From here there were more views across the Volga. In the centre of the square, surrounded by a five feet high hedge and lawn, is a 10 metre high sculpture monument, built in 1932, in memory of a Red Army commander, Vasily Ivanovich Chapaev. It's an impressive work, of one of the most famous of

Soviet heroes, showing him commanding a mixed band of struggling Bolshevik soldiers.

Chapaev, born in a peasant log cabin, which is still preserved in his native village, in his twenties, joined the military in WW1. His bravery gained him the Cross of St. George, the Russian equivalent of a VC. He won it three times, and was made a Commander. After the war, in 1917 he joined the Revolutionary Bolsheviks. One night, in Kazakhstan, a group of 'White Army' Cossacks attacked his unit. Wounded, he tried to escape by swimming the Ural River but drowned at the age of 32 years. Chapaev's exploits have been romanticised in several books and made into a film that became Stalin's favourite. Chapaev's portraits show a heavily moustachioed man of slim build, intense face, wild eyes and charismatic daring. In his wildest imagining he could never have believed that one day a town would be named after him, that statues would commemorate him and his exploits, or a film made of his life.

Do your best to be the best and anything can happen. In Petersburg there is a statue of him and, unlike Lenin's and Stalin's, his is still there.

Beyond Chapaev Square is a yellow, ugly building and in front of it what appears to be a bus shelter is the entrance to Stalin's Bunker. It's just a show piece, because he never actually went there, he stayed in Moscow during the Second World War, living in his five, isolated, sumptuous Dachas.

I rang a buzzer at the formidable steel door entrance to the bunker. Eventually a short, stocky, sleepy, heavy Russian came to the equally heavy security door. He seemed an incongruous mixture of caretaker, gardener and racketeer, all in one, dressed untidily, with Soviet style arrogance of manner. He stared at me, surprised, as though to ask, what are you doing here? I asked if I could see inside the bunker. He seemed to understand my request in

English but replied in Russian, 'It is closed until three thirty'. Disappointed I walked away.

I have never met anyone who has been inside the bunker, none of the travel writers who had visited, were able to get inside, not even Galina or Sasha or Kate. I had to content myself with photos of its interior. Apparently the caretaker only accepts groups. If you are a lone tourist or family you just can't get access. Below ground the bunker is on seven levels with Stalin's intended quarters at the very bottom.

Samarans, before 1991, had no idea this bunker existed. After the end of Communism it was revealed it had been built by convict gangs, working 120 feet below ground, then when it was finished the convicts who had worked on it were executed to ensure its secrecy. It's probably urban myth but under Stalin could well be true.

I walked back to the city centre to see the celebrated Samara railway station which I had read was an architecturally beautiful masterpiece but it too had gone. Built in 1876, like all Tsarist Railway Stations, it had been a delight of Gothic architecture but had been demolished in 1996. In its place a huge, glass greenhouse like structure, which would have suited Los Angeles more appropriately, has been built there.

Russia under Putin is modernising fast. By 2019 Russia will have high speed, bullet, trains whizzing by so rapidly you will wonder if you actually saw one. Russians have a way of getting things done without too much talk. In the West we fire ourselves up with "Walk the Talk" and "Can Do," attitude but Russians rarely publicise what they are going to do, they just get it done. It serves them well and all is accomplished, with artistic flair, in spite of corruption and their unpredictable temperament.

It was the kind of sultry day that encouraged indolence. Walking back to Chapaev Square I decided to visit Samara's Drama Theatre, located just beyond the Chapaev memorial, and drink kvass and coffee.

Samara's theatre is impressive, red brick and gothic, in a style Russians refer to as "Moscow Baroque" a design known for highly decorative, sombre exaggeration. This theatre, built in 1888, had been conceived by Mikhail Chichagov, a master architect, renowned for building theatres in Moscow and elaborate private theatres for rich merchant families.

Russians admire this building but I didn't find it attractive as I stared at its glaring red façade in the afternoon sunshine and thought it eerie and threatening, like some Hollywood vampire mansion. Art reflects society and at times is prophetic in imagery. The, Samara Drama Theatre design seemed a harbinger of the Communist terror about to unleash itself upon Russia's unsuspecting people. Chichagov sensing the mood of the time, Tsar Alexander 11 had been assassinated seven years before, intuitively reflected the approaching catastrophe in his building.

From Chapaev Square I walked, in sunshine, to Strukovsky Park, and ambled through an avenue of pale birches and then strolled to another nearby park, where I found a seat, overlooking the wide, delightful Volga and there rested.

The wonderful Volga River really does give an impression of being like a Russian Mother, expansive, slow, generous, nourishing, protecting, eternal and like all great rivers, mystical. As I sat watching it flow past it changed magically, moment by moment, relentlessly caught in an arrow of time that sought its demise in the indifferent Caspian Sea but this friendly river never dies. It is reborn forever in the magnificent Valdai Hills, 150 miles north west of Moscow. No one can see the Volga and not fall in love with her. Beyond the distant trees the river was serene, flowing reluctant, in her journey to the Caspian. There was barely a discernible breeze, sunlight danced from river to trees and onto neatly mown grass, creating a shimmering, ethereal, dreamlike radiance.

Life beside the Volga hasn't always been so blissful.

Before the revolution the Samara region had been known for producing the finest wheat in the world, yes the world, and along with Ukraine was the world's greatest exporter of grain. Of course perfidious nature often intervened, as it always does, with vagaries of Russia's summers and winters, Samara's Volga region was occasionally plagued by severe famines and crop failures. One such famine occurred in 1873-74 and another of even greater severity in 1891-92 and for this one Leo Tolstoy openly blamed the Tsarist Government and Orthodox Church for it. This famine, which began along the Volga, proliferated as far as the Ural Mountains. A dry autumn followed by a minus 31c winter was considered the reason. Russia had enough grain, to feed its people, but instead of easing their famine the Russian government chose to export the grain. Russians began organising anti-famine groups. Leo Tolstoy himself formed one but the Orthodox Church banned the devout, hungry, peasants from accepting his charity because he had openly criticised the Church.

The people's anger, simmering below the surface of unbearable, harsh existence, was ready to boil over. Peasants who should have been enjoying the produce of their labour were reduced to eating what became known as 'famine bread' made of suet, tree bark, husks and wild plants. Fourteen to twenty million people were affected, almost half a million died. It was avoidable and it incensed Tolstoy. The future Tsar, Nicholas 11, to his praise, did his best by raising approximately 7.5 million roubles, a huge sum and effort, to help his starving peasants. America also did whatever it could, to relieve this Russian famine, by shipping grain at a cost estimated, in today's money, at approximately $250 million.

These agricultural catastrophes, bad enough under the Tsars, were nothing compared to the ruthless, deliberately engineered, famines of Communist Russia. Lenin believed Russia's peasantry were attempting to disrupt his Bolshevik Revolution by withholding grain and farm produce from the Red army. There was some truth in this. Farmers were not convinced Revolution was a good thing for them.

The winter of 1921-2 was exceptionally severe. Lenin's Red Army needed to requisition food from reluctant peasants, so he decided to punish them. Armed guards of the dreaded Cheka were sent to torture and execute peasants accused of hiding their produce. It became large scale terror. In order to relieve this famine the revered Pokrovsky Cathedral, once shining, with marble and gold, and resplendent with icons and art was forced to sell its treasures to Finland for 32 carts of bread. God himself must have wept.

Among those who suffered most severely were the respectable, hardworking and religious, Volga Germans. In 1763, the German born Catherine the Great invited Europeans to settle in Russia and many German families, hardworking Lutherans, settled along the Volga River where they prospered due to a strong work ethic and close religious communities. In Lenin's opinion they opposed the Communist Revolution. To punish these bourgeoisies a Polish Jew, Felix Dzerzhinsky, was given the task of creating the sadistic, dreaded, murderous Cheka which later evolved into the notorious and even more feared KGB.

Dzerzhinsky set up office in what became known as the Lubyanka. Under his direction organised terror became the policy of the day. Germans, and peasants, were raped, shot, interrogated, tortured, executed and drowned in the Volga.

Another famine, this one intentionally engineered under Stalin, came in 1932. This time 350,000 Volga Germans perished as a result. By this time Communism, never about equality, had become a dictatorial oligarchy that Russians either embraced or became cannon fodder for a megalomaniac few.

This appalling attempt at genocide, like all injustices, had its repercussions. Hitler claimed that under Lenin and Stalin, Bolshevik Jews had massacred peaceful Germans along the Volga Basin and the Ukraine. In retaliation he vowed to exterminate them in return.

Russian writers have described, the mass murderer, Dzerzhinsky as having the face of a Russian Saint but whenever I have looked at his portraits all I see is the face of a gaunt, troubled lunatic. He died in middle age, which was no doubt a good thing, and should have been forgotten, seen as a blight on the human race, but people are perverse in judgment. A gigantic commemorative statue of him was raised in front of Moscow's notorious, torture chamber, the Lubyanka Prison. Dzerzhinsky's statue was justly removed at the collapse of Communism and that should have been that but now forty five per cent of Muscovites have requested it be returned.

Time doesn't heal everything, but helps us forget, and on this lovely day the Volga was gently peaceful.

Saturday came, Galina wanted us to go by ferry across the Volga to Zhiguli hills. It was a wonderful calm day, the air brisk and clear, the river expansive, as we boarded an old and tired looking vessel that contrasted miserably with splendid Volga cruise ships idling at the quay.

Not wanting to sit inside, on such a lovely sunny day, we leaned on ferry deck rails to observe life along the river. There were half a dozen travellers doing the same that day.

Quite unexpectedly a tall man came over to me and asked in an American accent, 'Are you English?'

'Yes.'

'I caught your voice. I'm American. This is my wife.' He introduced a reserved smiling woman in her late thirties.

They weren't the usual, immaculately preened, American travellers I was so used to.

'Are you touring?' I asked.

'No we work here. I'm with an American aid charity.'

Both appeared dejected, worn down by life in Russia and possibly an insufficient salary. I should have questioned them further but didn't.

'Do you have an office?' I asked.

'Yes, in a hotel on Volsky Prospect.'

I had noticed it near Galina's flat.

'Come along some time, we can talk.' He invited me and wrote his phone number in a small notebook, tore out the page, and gave it me, then returning to his taciturn wife they stared silently, over the rail on the opposite side of the ferry. She was American too, and for some reason reluctant to speak with us.

The river flung its ripples angrily along the ferry sides to join the rumbling, aged sound, of the ferry engine. Ahead of us a large cargo vessel passed, lifting a buffeting waves. On the Samara side of the river I could see, and became fascinated by, the exclusive grandeur of water front houses. One, a small palace from Tsarist days, was fronted by two enormous marble elephants, looking towards the river, that were too distant to guess their height but they were larger than life. Galina knew nothing about the palace and I conjectured it was now the home of some Russian oligarch or perhaps former Communist Party leader. Communism expounded equality but Party members were unashamedly more equal than others.

More Cargo vessels chugged the river; a few yachts were sailing near the shore. We were coasting towards Zhiguli Nature Reserve but our dilapidated, ponderous ferry would be there for one hour before returning to the city and it wouldn't leave much time to see anything. Eventually arriving at a wooden jetty, ahead of us was a small, oily beach on which bare chested men and bikini clad women sprawled, and scampered with children, taking the sun.

A steep, rubble path, beyond the untidy beach, led to a narrow country lane and on this, a quarter mile into our walk, laying back from the dirt road, stood a once magnificent Tsarist wooden house that had falling into disrepair and was now being restored by its fortunate new owner. Throughout Russia these once stately, centuries' old mansions, of Imperial landed gentry, have been neglected. Many lie empty in remote overgrown fields and birch forests.

Wooden Churches, unequalled in their skilfully improvised design, lie empty and derelict. We passed one of these, on the side of a deserted road, with bell tower still intact, and a forever silent bell hanging forlorn for all to see.

When Germany invaded Russia, during the Second World War, German soldiers became melancholic and despondent at the vast unending expanse of the Russian plain. Roads were not surfaced or signposted as in Europe.

Reluctant, disoriented Germans, frequently wandered off these rain soaked, ancient beaten tracks. No one had told them that Russian Church bells not only called villagers to worship but also functioned as sign posts on the eternal ocean of Russia's monotonously, horizontal wilderness, or that these Church bells sounded their resonating calls for miles as distinctly and clearly as beams from a lighthouse on a wild and desolate ocean.

A tarmacked lane gave way to become a wide bridle path. To my delight a horse drawn wooden cart, with that enormous bow shaped yoke and harness, favoured by the Slavs, passed us on the road. I was hoping we would see old, wooden villages but with only one hour to spare, before returning to the ferry, we never reached one. Galina was quiet, hidden within her own thoughts, perhaps tired in her persistent illness, I reasoned. Like all Russians, no matter how weary, she kept going with unshakeable fortitude. Anyone spending time with Russians sooner or later begins to admire their determined persistence, their ability to endure, their stoic acceptance of all that life throws at them. Not knowing this was Hitler's downfall and defeat. If he had known he would never have sent his military onto Russia's boundless plains.

On our return I was surprised the American couple were not on the last ferry back to Samara.

One Morning Galina suggested we visit Iversky Women's Monastery, not far from her apartment. This monastic building didn't look at all Russian. Founded in 1850, with a 230 feet high belfry it once housed some 500 nuns, mostly daughters of Samara's rich merchants. It all ended with the 1917 Revolution. In 1925 the monastery became a home for workers of the Zhiguli beer factory. It exposed the priorities of the Bolshevik mind with its penchant for insulting the once deeply religious life of the people. With the fall of

Communism it has become a monastery again. Inside we walked down a flight of stone steps to a small desk at which an ancient nun, frail and lonely, sitting in a corner without any window light to brighten her day, asked us to make a donation, which I did gladly. I asked if I could take photos but was refused. Throughout Russia, it is looked on as sacrilegious to take photos of, or in, any Churches or Monasteries.

In defiance, noticing a remarkable painting, on a flight of stairs, in another part of the monastery, I took a photo. We were the only visitors. The only other person there, apart from the aged desk assistant, was a cleaner, similarly downcast and forlorn, so absorbed with her floor mopping, of cold stone tiles, she never looked up or noticed us. She could easily have been mistaken for a ghost, forever wandering these monastery halls, oblivious to everything except her endless rounds. On display near the entrance were candles and icons for sale. Looking at the icons I noticed one bearing the image of the last Tsar, Nicholas 11, and another one of his Royal family.

'Galina that is the Tsar,' I said in surprise.

'No it can't be,' Galina doubted looking more closely.

When I insisted it was the Tsar Galina asked the nun, sitting behind the small desk. To Galina's surprise she confirmed Tsar Nicholas II and his family and all the servants assassinated with them, on that awful day were now canonized. I purchased two of these memorable icons.

Outside of the dismal monastery Galina suggested I meet her mother. We walked to a broad traffic island, on a busy street, which after crossing led to a narrow side street and the entrance to a dilapidated block of flats. Climbing narrow stairs we knocked on her mother's door. Galina's mother, a sprightly, robust Russian opened it to greet us.

There couldn't have been a greater contrast to Galina's own flat than this one. The room we entered was about ten by twelve feet with a single bed against one wall and an old, cheap wardrobe against the other leaving only about two feet between them. At the back I could see a toilet door and basin but no shower anywhere. For cooking there was a small stove in one corner. Galina's mother looked at me and I could see written in her eyes the shame she felt at her circumstances.

'Sasha got this place for my mother,' Galina said.

What Galina didn't say was that her mother had once lived in a much better Soviet flat but, at perestroika, unscrupulous, nefarious New Russians, that Putin later tried to deal with, unsuccessfully. The same ones Tony Blair, after George Bush had refused them entry into America, welcomed into England. These soon to be oligarchs had conned Russian people into selling their properties at paltry prices, sometimes with a real threat of violence, and not just their homes but their shares in factories and State owned businesses that Boris Yeltsin had handed back to the people. It seemed obvious Galina's mother had been one of the innocents.

Was that how Sasha had become so prosperous? I wondered.

Galina had studied at Samaras Medical University intending to become a doctor. Samara's Medical School, had been founded by Communists in 1919, and was in 1930 renamed Kuibyshev Medical Institute. By 1993 it had become one of the largest Medical Universities in Russia and was renamed Samara State Medical University.

After one year, and much reflection, Galina had decided medicine was not for her so changed her degree course to Economics and Finance. After mentioning this Galina said, 'I want to take you to see something interesting.'

The weather had changed, to grey, when we set off for Chapaevskaya Street where the Medical University is located but instead of entering the University Galina took me to a building that had once been a former Tsarist Jail but was now transformed into a Student Hall of Residence. At the entrance a porter, herself a doctor doubling her duties from lecturing, welcomed us politely with generous smile. Galina explained she had been a former pupil and wanted to show me the building and also asked for permission to see Valerian Kuibyshev's prison cell. The porter disappeared into her office and returned with a robust key and gave it to Galina.

The Halls of Residence still looked like a jail but doors to the former inmate cells were less severe. The cold, steel stairs remained and one couldn't deny the prison like atmosphere still pervading throughout. Central spaces were surrounded by a threatening gallery of locked doors and cast iron pillars.

Russia's Tsars, unlike the Bolsheviks, encouraged a compassionate, often lenient, judicial system in which they often commuted sentences and granted reprieves. Punishments were humane, without the brutal beatings, torture, or bullet in the back of the head that prevailed under Communism.

Kuibyshev, a revolutionary hero, guilty of insurrection against the Tsars, had been incarcerated in this Prison. Galina waited silently by my side while I gazed around, before leading me up a flight of steel steps to an austere gallery and to a wooden door, unlike the others, much older, stronger and built for security. Putting the heavy key into the lock she let me enter first.

We stood in a room, eight feet by twelve, that was frozen in time. Near a high window, that gave little light, was a desk against a wall, a single bed, and near the door a table. On the whole I thought not a bad place to be imprisoned. This small room had been Valerian Kuibyshev's prison cell in 1912 but such was life in Tsarist prisons his sister was allowed to visit and bring him extra food, cigarettes and sometimes a bouquet of flowers, and no doubt alcohol because Kuibyshev was known for an excessive consumption of vodka. It didn't seem at all bad punishment for a man that had planned to overthrow the government and get rid of the Tsar.

Before his revolutionary activities, the cultured, intelligent Kuibyshev had been a medical student, and later an accomplished musician and poet. He rose rapidly in the Communist hierarchy soon becoming a member of the Soviet Politburo. He died of heart failure and alcoholism at the early age of forty seven.

Punishment was never to be as congenially civilised again. Now Communism has ended serious crime means years in cruel confinement, and such lonely isolation that prisoners kill themselves or go mad.

On a small table near the door was a visitor's book. Galina opened it to scrutinise previous visitors but with Russian innate secrecy didn't sign it and didn't want me to either.

From the Student Halls we visited a large house on Frunze Street, the home of Alexei Tolstoy one of Russian most famous authors, at least in the eyes of the Communists. In the West he is known mainly by his autobiographical 'Nikita's Childhood,' a story of life in this very house. Alexei was a relative of the more famous Leo Tolstoy and on the maternal side of the family to the writer Ivan Turganev. Tsarist Russians, like all European landowners, mostly married into their own class. I suppose it was inevitable, with such celebrated literary relatives, he would turn to writing as a career. His father, a Count, Hussar, rake, libertine and duellist had been forced to leave his regiment. His wife abandoned him, unable to put with his wild temperament any longer, and took their baby Alexei with her. This was most likely the reason Alexei was cynical of all in authority seeing them as too controlling. He hated his father as much as his mother did.

Our childhood experiences lock us in cupboards for the rest of our lives.

The mansion house, so called in guide books, didn't appear mansion like at all. I told myself this was Russia. We walked to the entrance, on an overgrown garden path, to be greeted by husband and wife custodians. We were the only visitors. The man was polite, pleased to have us there, but strangely didn't seem to be an authority on Alexei Tolstoy and couldn't answer all the questions I asked him. We were shown first editions of Tolstoy's works, and his rooms, but weren't told that the writer had only lived there until his thirteenth year. On the wall were some photos of Alexei but the furniture appeared to be of a later date than when the writer lived there. Our guide showed us a Tolstoy's 19th century piano and I was invited to play on it if I wished.

Galina, herself from Samara, was completely ignorant of whom Alexei Tolstoy was, no doubt because since the fall of Communism he has fallen out of favour. He is now considered nothing more than a crony of Stalin. Alexei's life shows he certainly was that. He wrote voluminously, plays and novels he knew Stalin would approve of. His critics, since the demise of Communism, can say openly he had none of the values of Leo Tolstoy. They considered him a man without any social, or moral, character. This I believe unfair. Alexei didn't consider himself a reformer, as the more famous Leo had, and he lived in a much more dangerous time. I don't think Leo Tolstoy would have survived under Stalin, but Alexei did, by being all things to all men, a man determined to endure. He praised Stalin as a great leader, even if he didn't believe it and was awarded The Stalin Prize, the highest honour of Soviet times.

Alexei is also considered one of the first ever Sci-fi writers. An asteroid was named after him in 1974, confirming he knew how to live on when others didn't. If that isn't remarkable survival, under one of the most brutal political regimes ever, then what is? Others writers, such as Solzhenitsyn, ended up in Gulags but not crafty Alexei. I felt like taking a bow to him in his troubled childhood home.

Few nations take sport as seriously as Russians. Galina wanted me to see the renowned Samara Sport Complex. Stalin believed Communists should be perfect men and women and like Hitler believed that to achieve it one needed the rigorous discipline of sport. A person's philosophy always exposes what the person wants to be, but rarely are, and neither Hitler or Stalin were known for any sporting excellence.

Galina took me to a sports stadium the size of which I had never seen before with such an immense variety of gyms, swimming pools, tennis courts, tracks and pitches I couldn't possibly have visited them all.

Weary from walking this huge sport arena we relaxed in a smallish café to rest and drink coffee. Four soldiers entered, one of whom must have been seven feet tall and so broad of shoulder he not only ducked his head but also had to turn sideways to enter the café. The other three soldiers were all above six feet four tall and each as robust as a military tank.

Galina, seeing my surprise, started laughing.

'Not unusual here,' she said through her humour.

'No wonder Russians were able to annihilate the Nazi's army,' I replied.

'Who would attack the Russian Bear?' my father, who had been a soldier, once commented when discussing World War 11 and the answer is of course 'No one in their right mind.' It is now accepted that eighty per cent of the German army was destroyed, not by British, French or Americans but by Russians. It has taken fifty years for the West to acknowledge it was Russia that won the Second World War.

Not only physically formidable Russians are also remarkable in their endurance and patient, determined, persistence. I have known them travel, for days, sitting on cramped trains, on hard seats, without complaint, and seen them waiting on freezing railway stations for hours, or even days, at a time, and taking it in their stride. They endure whatever life, nature or time, throws at them with humble fortitude and remarkable resolution.

Russians not only carry vodka but also books in their pockets and are forever learning. They may not always be nice people to know but you end up loving and admiring them anyway.

Our café experiences were not always so pleasant. One sunny day Galina and I, visiting an old part of Samara to look over its market stalls on a quiet street, entered a respectable looking café. At the door we were confronted by a man, in military uniform, who proceeded to search Galina's handbag and purse before we were allowed to sit down. He made no attempt to search me. The café was empty; at the rear stood two neatly attired, pretty, teenage waitresses looking apprehensively afraid. One of them came over and we ordered coffee and a light meal. When the bill came it was three times what we would normally pay. Galina remonstrated with them but they shrugged their shoulders quietly and uneasily.

Outside, after our overpriced lunch, Galina explained Mafia gangs demanded a cut from businesses for protection money. The soldier was there either as part of such a gang, or to protect the owner, or possibly just to force closure of the business so someone could acquire it illegally and inexpensively.

I was to see more of these protection rackets during my stay in Russia. It was one of the ways Russian billionaire oligarchs, living in Europe to escape Putin, had acquired their enormous wealth.

Galina had struggled with illness for years. She hadn't accepted it passively. Each morning she rose early, exercised, jogged, walked, or played tennis, and followed a strict diet. Sadly, it helped little. Some days she lay down, her heart dangerously unsteady, yet she never missed a day of work and I grew to admire her uncomplaining stoicism.

Time arrived for me to leave this generous Russian family I had grown to love. I rang the youthful looking Dean of Yaroslavl University, whom I had met on the London to Moscow flight. She remained indelible in my memory as a woman of thirty five who looked eighteen. Over time I learned this isn't unusual in modern Russia, where women are frugal eaters, often active in sport or dance, and walk everywhere and this helps prolong their youthfulness.

'Oh! Yes of course I remember you, please come and visit us, and my parents in Yaroslavl, whenever you can. I will be busy most days but my daughter will gladly show you the city. You can stay at my parents. Let me know when you arrive in Moscow and then I will tell you where the Yaroslavl train can be caught.' Svetlana replied enthusiastically.

When I told Galina, she thought for a moment and suggested, 'Well, I have a good friend in Petersburg, who will be pleased to help you. Instead of Moscow go first to Petersburg. Meet her, for a day or two, then catch one of the all night trains to Yaroslavl. You will like our sleeper trains, much better than yours I believe and cheaper.'

Not wishing to contradict or disagree, I answered, 'What a lovely idea.'

'I will ring my friend in Peters and maybe she will meet you at the airport OK?'

'Are you sure?' All this trouble on my behalf didn't seem such a good idea to me.

'Well you will eventually have to see Peters and she will help you with accommodation and sightseeing. Believe me when you meet her you won't regret it at all.' Galina laughed, then added, 'Give her one hundred dollars per week as your guide because she hasn't a job at the moment and is in Peters visiting her family.'

After a few phone calls everything was agreed.

'You will recognise me, five feet nine, brown hair, wearing a yellow suit. My name is Marina,' she said.

'Right,' I agreed, finally convinced.

Kate and Olga, as a farewell dinner, prepared a traditional Russian meal for us in their luxurious, Samara apartment. Expensive electronic equipment was everywhere; their large bathroom, the most opulent I had ever seen, had gold framed, gem studded mirrors and there were spacious wash basins with gold plated taps. It seemed a millionaire retreat.

We drank vodka and traditional salted bread before our dinner. During dinner conversation I was warned by Galina, 'In Russia you must not speak politics.'

Putin had warned businessmen 'Don't get involved in Politics.' Sasha was especially vulnerable, not only was he a successful businessman but also a former politician. On the day we said our goodbyes he couldn't come with us to the airport but arrived early with Olga to say farewell and he signalled me to ring them.

Galina wanted to accompany me, on the one hour drive at 4.00 am, to catch a flight to Peters leaving at 5.30 am. She insisted even though on her return to Samara she would still have to go to her bank employment. I gave them parting gifts, in appreciation of their generosity, but with a feeling they were inadequate. Galina I caught a taxi to the airport, the loneliest ride I have ever taken, as we passed through the dark, damp forests and Galina tired and unusually silent.

Galina sat beside me in the airport lounge until my flight was called, and watched over the wooden departure barrier, until I had to board my flight.

I told her to leave before this but kissing my cheek she replied, 'No! Sometimes we say goodbye to friends and never see them again.'

This was to be prophetic because I never saw any of them again. Galina I believe joined her husband in Cyprus, or somewhere else, but wherever it was I was never able to find them.

Now, at the mercy of airport staff, I came across Russia's official propensity to rob foreigners of all they could. During the months ahead I was to experience it many times and often at airports.

Looking at my passport a desk clerk scowled, weighed my bags and told me to pay an extra $100 more. I was sure my bags were much lighter than when I came. This heavy boned, morose, clerk, with the appearance and demeanour of a Stalinist bully gave me a slip of paper and, with disgust contorting her face, pointed to another dour clerk across the room, who took my money.

In concern for me at the hands of these bureaucratic gangsters, Galina, observing it all, from the lounge partition, seemed prepared at any moment to angrily intervene. When I finally left, to board my flight to Petersburg, she waved. That was the last I ever saw of her.

REVOLUTION ROAD

On the flight to Petersburg the seat next to mine was occupied by a musician from Cleveland Ohio Orchestra, considered one of the best orchestras in America, listed in America's top five. He was on his way to play in Petersburg. I found him sociable, intelligent and with such an excellent knowledge of Petersburg, a city he loved, he was able to tell me the best places to visit.

At Petersburg Pulkovo airport I was met by Galina's friend, a tall, smiling, truly beautiful woman in cream coloured suit holding a sign above her head that displayed my name in Capital letters. Standing beside her was a girl of eleven years holding a red rose that she presented to me in greeting.

Our taxi to the city, took forty five minutes, I explained to my host Marina I had found an apartment to rent, for a few days, at $40 per night.

'Oh, that is too much. I can get one much cheaper for you. Perhaps better also,' Marina smiled, delighted she could help me.

From our taxi window she pointed out places of interest while Lara, her daughter, watched me intently. Arriving at Nevsky Prospect, Petersburg's most famous thoroughfare, Marina rang a friend then turning to me said, 'I have a place for you, a large apartment, $20 per night near the city centre. Would you like to see it?'

Marina's English was excellent, her daughter Lara's even better. Since the fall of Communism all children in Russia are taught English, as a second language, and many wealthy Russian parents engage English tutors teach them.

We crossed the wide Neva River, Petersburg's great Palaces skirting its banks and city boulevards; ferries wended along Petersburg's historic canals. We reached Petrogradskaya, one of the most exclusive parts of Petersburg and alighted at Lenina, a street built between 1905 -1911, a place where once lived Petersburg's pre-Revolution middle classes.

At the demise of Imperial Russia these large dwellings became homes of Soviet bureaucrats, medalled athletes and Soviet business directors. Under Stalin the finest of these residences were allotted to members contributing most to Soviet ideals.

The apartment we entered, belonging to a former Russian Olympic swimming champion, was luxuriously spacious, clean, well-furnished and with 1600 square feet had ample room for the three of us. I noticed the outside walls were eighteen inches thick, as they had been in Galina's apartment in Samara but these were un-shuttered. In one room hung a portrait of Putin, the majority of Russians admire and support him, a reputed 80 per cent of the population. In one corner there was an old, much worn icon, of a silent saint set in a frame. The apartment had two bedrooms, two living rooms and reasonable size kitchen with a dining table for four.

From the window, across a broad street, I could see an office with a derogative comment, painted brightly in large orange letters, explaining the owner of that office was a Jew. It was my first instance of open anti-Semitism in Russia. Sasha, the Samaran businessman had told me Jews were hated in Russia for fleecing the people after the fall of Communism.

Marina's husband, a Colonel in the Russian Army and an acquaintance of Putin, was stationed in Moscow for the time being, but their flat there was quite small. She showed me his photo in full military uniform, slim, tall, a handsome man, standing beside Putin.

Staring proudly at the photo Marina exclaimed, 'One day soon he will be a General.'

Turning to look at me more closely she said, 'Galina told me all about you. I am in Peters visiting our relatives, if you don't mind me and Lara could stay with you to make sure you are safe and have all you need.'

'Of course, there's plenty of room.'

'We have our own awful apartment here but it's in the poorest area. I owned it before meeting my husband.'

Military personnel in Russia are paid poorly and infrequently. It was clear Marina was grateful for any money she could earn, acting as my guide, to help her and Lara.

Lara, Marina's daughter smiled. She was a remarkable girl, pretty, with hazel eyes and light brown hair, caring and happy and I soon realised extremely intelligent. At eleven years she was tall, slim, athletic, and spoke superb English and had already won several swimming medals.

Two floors below our apartment, at street level, a small supermarket sold produce and household items so once I'd settled in, my clothes sorted from suitcases, we went down to buy food.

In the evening I decided to visit Petersburg's famous Nevsky Prospekt.

Close by my apartment was Chkalovskaya Metro. No country has such remarkable metros as Russia. Outside this one was a fifty feet high mural covering the whole wall. In front of the metro entrance, on a plinth, was a bust of the Russian Aviator, Valery Chkalov, in a pilots helmet.

Chkalov was one of Russia's most famous pilots and the first man ever to fly over the North Pole to America. American President, Roosevelt, had met him at the end of the journey to honour him, in Washington, before the start of

World War 11.

I saw photos of Chkalov's plane in which he had flown this epic journey, for those days, from Moscow to America. It was truly beautiful and elegantly designed with long red wings that made it graceful as a seabird.

Chkalov died in a crash, testing a new type of aircraft for Russia, but he was not forgotten. Russians never forget their heroes. The Chkalov Metro in Petersburg is a memorial to him. It isn't the only one; there are several other metros that honour his achievements and in Vancouver, Canada, there is a monument at the spot he first landed his plane after his record flight.

Outside, in appearance, the metro was not remarkable but inside it was captivating, two hundred feet below ground level, it was lit by wall lights resembling the turning blades of an aircraft. The metro hall was reminiscent of an airport lounge. At one end of it is displayed a man with arms raised, surrounded by colours radiating around him, like a modern icon. This metro is everything London tube stations are not.

It was a delightful place for me to observe Russians engaging with life and each other. If you really want to accustom yourself to Russian people spend an hour, in a Russian metro hall, just watching. This evening my destination was Gostiny Dvor on Nevsky Prospekt.

Gostiny Dvor, meaning Merchants Inn, is an enormous department store, originally begun in the time of Catherine the Great, to house and sleep traders, who came from all over Europe as well as Russia to sell goods in Petersburg. Initially built of wood it inevitably burned down but was reconstructed, over a twenty four year period, in stone. Like all buildings, of Catherine's, found in St. Petersburg it is quite spectacular.

This gigantic, yellow building, with a frontage one kilometre in length has two tiers of arcades supported by countless columns. Its arched walkways protect buyers and sellers from all that Russian winters can throw at them. Inside it is an enormous shopping mall, selling everything imaginable. Crowded with people, buying and window shopping, its galleries are framed by broad arches lit by elegant globe lights.

Gostiny Dvor is impressive, spotlessly clean with an endless riot of halls selling jewellery, produce, designer clothes, souvenirs and everything you would ever need, all gleamingly displayed. In case you feel carried away by this variety of splendour, just to remind you this is Russia, everywhere stand dark suited, watchful, heavy-weight men with no-nonsense stares.

I had arrived in Petersburg at the time of its celebrated White Nights when, due to its northern location, light never leaves the sky. At 11 pm on Nevsky it was like mid- day.

Leaving Gostiny I noticed, down a small street, a blue and white building resembling a mock Greek temple that seemed to deliberately shrink from the crowds. It was an Armenian Church, more than two hundred years old, built by a famous Armenian Jeweller and paid for after selling an enormous diamond to one of Catherine's many lovers, Count Orlov, who graciously gave it to her as a gift.

There was always a large Armenian community in Petersburg from its early beginnings. In appreciation of them, and their piety, Catherine had given them this plot for their church. It wasn't possible at that time of night to enter the Church so I left for home.

The next day I decided to visit the tourist crowded 'Church on Spilled Blood' and stroll Nevsky Prospekt Petersburg's main thoroughfare, built on the orders of Peter the Great as a road to join Novgorod to Moscow. Since then Nevsky has become one of the most famous roads in the world, in one of the most beautiful cities ever built. I was charmed by its wide roads, palaces, gardens and cafes.

Turning off Nevsky I walked beside Griboedova Canal. From there to the Church on Spilled Blood, one of the most striking buildings I had ever seen. Glistening in the morning sun, like some elaborate Faberge creation, it had been designed by an English architect, born in Petersburg, named Alfred Parland. You soon realise you need binoculars to take it all in; there is so much detail on its façade that is out out of reach, high and distant. The name 'Church on Spilled Blood' itself explains part of the story of this remarkable structure.

In 1881 Tsar Alexander II, a kindly, reforming Tsar, was assassinated on this spot. There had already been five previous attempts on his life, by revolutionaries, over a fifteen year period. On this final attempt they were determined to accomplish it. Three assassins were present just to make sure at least one of them would succeed. A first bomb thrown failed to kill the Tsar so a second was hurled that blew his legs to pulp. It was one of those sad, unnecessary, events that proliferate constantly through the timeline of Russian history.

Alexander was not an oppressive ruler and was far more aware of the aspirations of his subjects than any other Russian Tsar before him or after and dedicated himself to listening to the anger of discontent rolling across the vastness of his empire. On 3rd March 1861 Alexander had issued, 'The Manifesto to Emancipate the Serfs,' intending to free Russia's twenty three million serfs who for centuries had been tied to a land system that amounted to slavery. The words of his Manifesto stated, "It is a sacred mission that Divine

Providence has called upon us to fulfil."

When this proclamation was made public, crowds stood in front of the Winter Palace cheering but It wasn't long before this cheering, and celebration, changed to cries of despair. Fine details, in the four hundred pages Manifesto, stated that the land, Serfs had hoped would be given to them after centuries of toil on their small holdings, would have to be purchased by them. There would be a two year interim waiting period then Serfs, who had very little wealth of their own, would be given eighty per cent loans, at a six per cent interest, over a forty nine year period to buy their land. Basically that meant Serfs would still be tied to landowners, during that period, until their debt was paid. When the offer was taken up, by the more affluent Serfs, if they missed payments, due to bad harvests, the Tsar's Police and Military were sent to enforce repayment.

Alexander hadn't gone far enough in his reforms and would pay for it with his life. Twenty years after the Manifesto, to the month, Alexander was assassinated near Pevchesky Bridge. The first bomb only injured the Tsar's Cossack guards and true to his nature Alexander got out of his carriage, against advice, to help his wounded men then a second bomb was thrown at him destroying his legs and stomach.

Alexander II is considered one of the most successful of reforming Russian monarchs. In addition to attempting to emancipate Serfs he had also abolished Capital Punishment. If the assassins had waited just two more days Russia would also have had its own elected parliament. Alexander had already written up its proposal, and signed it, but not yet presented it to the people. Had he lived Russian history would have been entirely different, with a constitutional monarchy, as in England, and probably no Revolution.

As a young man Alexander had been a suitor of England's Queen Victoria but she, fortuitously, preferred the more handsome Prince Albert. Photos of Alexander show him a man troubled, tired, burdened with grief, struggling as he faced the restless march of Revolution.

It is often quoted, "The evil that men do lives after them; the good is oft interred with their bones," and this is certainly true of Alexander II. Much that he tried to achieve for the Russian people would have been forgotten except for this magnificent 'Church on Spilled Blood'. It isn't really a church at all. hardly any services are held there, it is an opulent mausoleum, as grand in its Slavic way as the Taj Mahal.

Alexander III in 1883, two years after his father's murder, commissioned this monumental tomb to be built and in anger, at the murder of his father, reversed his father's reforms believing Russia required strong, not liberal, rulers.

Like many acts of terrorism this assassination had the opposite effect to the one intended.

At the entrance to the Church I was charged, as a foreigner, a fee eight times more than Russians. Inside this Christmas cake edifice you immediately become aware of being in a tomb; with tremendously high, vaulted ceilings, wide spaces devoid of comfort, and no seats. Everywhere there is exuberance of colour, reflecting from over twenty different types of semi-precious stone mosaics, that cover floors, walls and ceilings. It is one of the largest mosaic collections in the world, covering 7000 square metres, created by artists from Petersburg's Academy of Fine Arts and this remarkable mosaic floor is all of Italian marble.

Stalin, in hatred of all things ecclesiastic, closed the Church to services and turned this wondrous building into a storage warehouse. It was not opened again to the public, after extensive restoration, until August 1997.

The outside of the Church is just as remarkable as inside. On its bell tower there are coats of arms of all Russia's towns and provinces. Lower down are scenes from Alexander II's reign. Above and beneath its Byzantine, turban domes, are scenes from Alexander II's reign and above and beneath these are portraits of the Saints of Russian Orthodoxy.

This amazing building, constructed over the very spot where Alexander was assassinated, took 24 years to complete. In the western part of the Church the exact place the Tsar had been fatally wounded is covered by a canopy and the original cobblestone pavement is preserved with the railings taken from the scene of the tragedy.

There is no sense of holiness in this giant, artistic monument. It fills you with a sense of confusion. Its lavish display must have indelibly scratched at the heart, of struggling Russians, with its testimony to the gap between rulers and ruled. It was such excess at the top that fuelled resentment and revolution.

From the Church I ambled along Griboedova. Tourist boats trafficked the canal. Speed boats troubled the mud coloured water. On Nevsky I turned right towards the Neva, passed the revered Lady of Kazan Cathedral then on to the most opulent residence in Petersburg, the Stroganov Palace, gleaming pinkish gold in the midday light.

The Stroganovs had been the wealthiest family in Russia. Their long history of achievements had commenced under Ivan the Terrible, long before Petersburg had been built. After 163 years of occupancy, of their extravagant Palace, the family lost it all in the 1917 Revolution and it is now part of The Russian Museum.

Pausing beside the Neva I stared across its shiny wide expanse. It is one of the shortest of rivers yet has the third largest discharge of water in Europe, fed by Lake Ladoga, 46 miles away, which pours its fabulous volume through Petersburg before empting into the Baltic. The Neva is wide and at 1600 feet twice as broad as the Thames in London. Across the river I could see the Menshikov Palace brightly tawny in the reflected light of day. One of the oldest palaces in St Petersburg it had been built for Alexander Menshikov, the tall, handsome, moustachioed friend and advisor to Peter the Great who, in gratitude, made him the first Governor of Petersburg.

To the left of Menshikov Palace is an even more impressive building, The Academy of Arts, built in 1757. In front of it, quite incredibly, facing the river, are two 3,500 year old Egyptian Sphinxes from the city of Thebes. The faces on these impressive monuments are of the most prosperous and successful of Egyptian Pharaohs, Amenhotep III. These sphinx should have gone to France but their revolution disrupted the purchase and once more they came up for sale. Nicholas I of Russia bought them in 1830.

Marina was a silent companion but the most observant person I ever met. She had an artist's eye for detail and perspective and a phenomenal memory. Any question I asked she answered accurately without hesitation. She was a superb artist with an unusual gift for colour and almost photographic detail in her work. Her personality was cold, cynical and indifferent to everyone, except her daughter. I often noticed she had a constant nervous movement in her long graceful fingers that told me she had experienced trauma at some point, in her troubled life that had left her with perpetual anxiety.

Walking down Nevsky I couldn't in any way imagine this road, in the days of Tsarist Russia, when it would have been filled with men in colourful uniforms, on restless horses, brightly liveried coachmen mounted on carriages or women in red, gold and blue embroidered dresses.

This exceptional road changed with time through the jostling, often tragic turbulence of Russian history. It was on this street, in 1905, that twenty thousand men, women and children led by a priest at the forefront, marched to the Tsar's Winter Palace. They carried an icon and a portrait of Tsar Nicholas, to show they meant him no harm, and a petition that said;

"We are in deepest poverty and oppressed with labours beyond our strength.-Things have become so terrible for us we would prefer death to the unbearable torment we are forced to suffer."

They came, they wrote, "only to ask the Tsar for justice and protection."

Their petition had stated they preferred death over torment and that is what Tsar Nicholas' soldiers gave them. Hundreds of these unharmed, and peaceful, marchers were fired on and slaughted, all on a bright, sunny morning.

Nicholas II wasn't even at the Winter Palace at the time; he had done what he always did, in times of crisis, fled to safety. The legacy of his grandfather's assassination haunted him and the rising discontent of his people left him inadequate for the task confronting him.

Nor could I imagine, on a similar lovely Petersburg day, in February 1917, police beating crowds, of starving people, with rifle butts and clubs. It was done frequently along this wide thoroughfare.

Things became so bad on Sunday 26th February that a quarter of a million people took to the streets and again were fired on by the Tsar's troops. Two hundred unarmed people, including children, died that day.

Revolutions arise because men at the top, obsessed by greed, refuse to distribute their privileged affluence, or share it, with the populace that created it.

Walking beside the indifferent, determined flow of the Neva we came to the Winter Palace, beyond the great archways of the General Staff Building. The two archways are splendid, topped with a thirty three foot tall sculpture of an angel, riding a chariot pulled by six horses. Passing beneath them one sees the expansive Palace Square, once the Tsar's parade ground, and the unforgettable Winter Palace on the far side.

In the centre of the square stands the tallest monument in the world, the Alexander I column, 156 feet high, topped also with an angel commemorating Russia's victory over Napoleon. Constructed out of red granite it glowed like a fiery pillar in the sunlight, a giant totem, telling the world, 'We are here to stay.'

The imposing, pale blue and white, Winter Palace was originally commissioned, and partially constructed, by Peter the Great. His daughter Elizabeth, in 1754, reconstructed and expanded it to publicise Russia's growing might on the world stage. Unintentionally, it revealed the ruthless gap between rich and poor, and flaunted the extravagant opulence of the nobility within Russia's Empire, just as the Palace of Versailles had done in France. Statistics reveal this beautiful building to be 650 feet long and 500 feet wide, with approximately 1050 rooms, 1786 windows, 117 staircases, and doors 40 feet high. If you wish to walk it's perimeter it is more than one mile. If you have the time, which most tourists don't have, you can walk through all of the exhibitions of 'The Hermitage', without stopping to see any. If you did you would have ambled thirteen miles in about four and a half hours. Not a bad idea if you want to keep fit in one of the most beautiful interiors ever created.

Hardly anything is written of Empress Elizabeth, Peter's daughter, who did much to design the Winter Palace; her great father Peter always dominates the accolades. After Elizabeth's death came Catherine the Great, who wasn't Russian at all, who out of admiration tried to emulate the remarkable Elizabeth.

Elizabeth was an iconic Russian beauty, tall, blonde, blue eyed, with long legs that were noted for their shapely seduction which she emphasised by dressing in the tight trousers of her cavalry officers. Empress Elizabeth was considered one of the prettiest women in the world and the ideal of Slavic feminine perfection. When she fell in love, at the age of 21, it was to a handsome peasant, a Cossack of 23 renowned for his admirable voice and who sang in the Imperial Choir. This fortunate young man was Alexei Razumovsky. Catherine the Great remarked he was the most handsome man she had ever seen. Alexei was also extremely pious, courteous, with no elevated ambitions, even when Elizabeth showered him with honours and palaces. They remained lovers all their lives and it was rumoured they had secretly married. Portraits of him remind me of Hollywood actors, Cornell Wilde and Tyrone Power.

Charming, beautiful, attention seeking Elizabeth was frivolous. She loved to party in fancy dress and was said to have a priceless collection of 1700 dresses and hundreds of shoes. She was also a compassionate ruler and an intelligent one. Her soldiers loved her bold, feisty, captivating, flirty, ways and especially that she was a renowned horse rider and huntress.

Elizabeth attempted to abolish the death penalty in Russia but her court refusing to do this she smartly refused to sign any execution orders and during her reign no one was executed. This hatred of severe punishment was perhaps because she had seen, and hated, her father's brutality. Life was never dull around, captivating, elegant, Elizabeth.

The Winter Palace, part of the Hermitage complex of six buildings, exhibits one of the greatest art collections in the world, holding approximately 300 million items, a number so huge only 5 per cent of the collection can be displayed at any one showing. This amazing collection, begun by Catherine the Great in 1764, soon needed an extension on the east wing of the Winter Palace then another extension, seven years later, so enormous had her Catherine's art treasure grown. Later Tsars added to this accumulation, Alexander I added more paintings and so did Nicholas I.   This entire, remarkable repository could have been lost, during the siege of Petersburg (Leningrad) by the Germans during World War II, except for the foresight of the Hermitage curators who moved this vast collection, rapidly and secretively to safety by train over the famous Ice Road.

One unusual aspect of the Hermitage, I believe most visitors are not aware of, is its number of cats. Empress Elizabeth introduced them from Kazan, where cats were supposed to be the best at catching mice. Ever since, except during the World War 11, these Hermitage cats have lived in its vast palatial complex, protecting invaluable art collections from nightly rodent destruction. Over the years their number has grown to around 74 and there is now an Hermitage basement department created to care for them, making sure all are neutered and fed. The museum now adopts some cats that need a home. In several visits, to the Hermitage, I never saw any perhaps they were dozing somewhere in the afternoon sun or were hidden away from visitors wanting to take one of them home.

It is impossible to describe the Hermitage collection, so vast that, after a short while, numbness settles on one's soul and you become tired with it all. Out of all these mind boggling displays,   from every corner of world, the ones that most lingered with me were those by Russia's own artists.

Leaving the Hermitage I walked to see Petersburg's famous, 'Bronze Horseman' in Senate Square. I'd read extensively about Peter the Great and, like everyone else who visits Petersburg, I wanted to see this famous equestrian statue.

Commissioned by Catherine this attractive sculpture which took twelve years to construct shows Peter galloping his horse, up a gigantic granite block, to point dramatically across the Neva. Peter's face was copied from his death mask, so is a good likeness, his body however is not so accurately depicted. Writers, from the time of his reign, described him as six feet eight inches tall, with spindly, thin legs and small head. The statue shows none of that.

This swaggering, statue of Peter is twenty feet high, resting on top of a granite block itself twenty five feet tall. The granite, on which the statue stands, is just as remarkable as Peter's bronze effigy. It is named, 'The Thunder Stone', because once upon a time it was struck by a lightning bolt that broke a large slice of it away, when it was still a massive chunk of granite near the Gulf of Finland. It is largest stone ever moved by men and was transported, on an enormous sledge rolling on metal spheres, to a great raft supported by warships built to float it to Petersburg. Approximately 400 men, without any animals involved, took nine months to bring it to its destination.

On top of this incredible mass of granite Peter's statue appears halted at a cliff edge with his raised hand pointing towards the Peter and Paul Fortress, which was where, in his attempt to gain access to the Baltic Sea, dominated at that time by the Swedish Empire, he had built his fortress. From that place he commenced to build his Russian Navy and was able to take on the Swedes and control the Baltic. To build his fleet he chose an Englishman, John Perry, a naval engineer, who successfully designed for Peter 300 warships, English style, to destroy the might of Sweden.

It was a determined aspiration. Russia fought Sweden for 21 years before Peter finally realised his ambition of controlling access to the Baltic Sea.

The following day I set off to visit this historic fort and crossed Trinity Bridge, recognised by its ten arches and famous lamp posts, to arrive at the fortress. Its walls were built by soldiers, and serfs, who did it without even the most elementary tools such as picks, shovels or barrows. This wall clutches the whole island in its grasp and when, in 1704, it was completed it was partially clad with a granite façade.

At the end of Trinity Bridge you pass through the white stone entrance of St John's Gate, dated 1740. Ahead lies St Peter's Gate, a superbly arched structure with the Russian double headed eagle, above it. Two niched sculptures, one of the Goddess Athena one side and the goddess of wisdom the other, welcome you in.

After passing this monumental gate, you notice the true attraction of the fortress, the Peter and Paul Cathedral with its 402 feet high needle spire.

This Cathedral was unlike any I had ever visited; gigantic chandeliers, green and pink columns, exuberant wall and ceiling paintings and like all cathedrals it is a mausoleum. Its white marble tombs are of the Romanov dynasty. The remains of Alexander 11, the assassinated Tsar, lie beneath a monument of red jasper and his wife beneath one of green marble.

In a side chapel, dedicated to St Catherine, lie remains of the last Tsar, Nicholas 11, his wife Alexandra and their children. Their bodies were exhumed from an Urals forest pit, into which they had been thrown like bundles of refuse by the Bolsheviks.

Peter the Great's own tomb rests close to a chandelier he is reputed to have helped make. He was always a hands on character happiest making and designing things himself, as he worked beside his craftsmen, so I believe this story true.

In spite of his love of the common man there was a side to Peter's complex personality that made him less likeable, he was often violent, joining in fist fights, at drunken banquets. Once, when dining, he struck one of his advisors so hard that blood spurted from the wound. At the age of 27, after ordering the execution of 57 of his rebellious Streltsy Regiment during which he joined in the slaughter, he forced many of them to endure the most viciously perverted forms of torture. Even before this display of pathological violence he was recorded as often beating his first wife, the frail and pretty Eudoxia and eventually banished her to a monastery because he found her boring. Their son, Alexei, was terrified of and hated his violent father intensely and Peter knew it. Alexei was finally tortured to death. Peter went to the fortress dungeons daily to observe the procedure.

This addiction to torture, murder and brutality creeps, like a destructive, untameable monster, throughout Russian history. Peter loved to bully and humiliate. At one of his palace balls an old courtier had been reluctant to wear the masquerade costume chosen for him. Peter had him stripped naked, put on an ice flow, in the middle of winter, on the River Neva, and left him there all night. The following morning the old man returned to his home where he lay down on his bed and died.

At only 52 years Peter himself died, after enduring two years of pain, of an infected bladder and kidney failure, and exhaustion from overstretching his unremitting, nervous energy. Probably everyone, who knew him well, was glad to see him go.

For all his madness, in twenty nine years, Peter transformed his backward nation into an empire, placed it forever on the stage of world power, developed seaports for his land locked country, built a navy to be proud of and created from swampland one of the most beautiful cities in the world.

My guide Marina at times seemed quite ill, not alert, as though suffering from depression but she didn't voice any complaint. Life is hard for many Russians. From the little she told me her life had been excessively traumatic and unbearably painful. She had lost her first husband, Lara's father, due to an avoidable tragedy, when he was thirty years old. Benefits, she received from the government for this loss, were free bus and train travel and free access to galleries, palaces and exhibitions. This is a sensible Russian way of providing equality, and education, for all children. These benefits cease when a child reaches 18 years.

A walk on the Peter and Paul fortress walls gives magnificent views over the Neva. Speed boats were racing around the fortress island. Below these massive walls, it being a hot, cloudless day, I could see bathers, reclining on the sands, resting pale bodies against its stone walls, capturing sunshine. None wore bathing suits; men reclined in pants and slacks, women in underwear, or open topped dresses, tanning their breasts.

For much of its existence the fortress was used not for naval purposes but as a notorious prison called 'The Trubetskoy Bastion' one of the most feared prisons in the Russian Empire and home to the Tsars feared secret police. Over the years Trubetskoy had seen the incarceration of Dostoyevsky, Gorky, Trotsky and Lenin's own brother Alexandr Ulyanov who was taken from here and hanged when he was just 21 years old.

92

Lenin never forgot this and was heard to say, 'I will make them pay for this, I swear it.' His determined pursuit of vengeance was equal to that of Sabatini's Scaramouche. He exacted the ultimate revenge on Nicholas 11, by wiping the whole Romanov dynasty off the face of the Earth, at Yekaterinburg, in 1918.

Inside, this hated institution, are 72 small cells, each side of long, dismally dark, corridors set on two levels. Each cell had a small window, high above, so prisoners couldn't see out or be seen suffering in a damp, cold misery. There was a torture chamber where inmates were given an unbelievable 8000 lashes, or 400 blows, solitary confinement and only bread and water to survive on.

The first inmate, incarcerated in this diabolical fortress prison, was Peter's own son Alexei. I asked an attendant to show me the chamber, in which Peter's son had been tortured, but was told it was no longer open to the public and was closed permanently. The idea of the Great Peter torturing his own son, to death, is no longer something 'New Russia' wishes to promote.

Alexei had been whipped daily with the barbaric Russian knout, a whip designed to rip flesh to the bone. Alexei's pregnant wife, Afrosina, was also held in this prison as his accomplice. She gave birth to their child, while there, but the baby, Peter's grandchild, was murdered on Peter's orders. After Alexei had died from torture, Peter set Afrosina free. She lived for a further thirty unhappy years.

With delight, from this same fortress the Bolsheviks, on the night of 25th Oct 1917, bombarded the Tsar's Winter Palace.

Leaving this place it was a relief to visit Peter's Log Cabin. Surrounded by iron railings and, protective, red brick façade, it is reputed to be the first house built in Petersburg. In 1703 soldiers of Peter's Semyonovsky Regiment, directly after their major victory over the Swedes, built it for him in just three days. The Semyonovsky were Peter's own, renowned regiment, formed by him when merely a boy and their loyalty to him was unshakeable. Communists, under Lenin, disbanded them in 1918 as being too Tsarist but recently Putin has re-established them, perhaps to reveal he is a new Tsar of all of Russia.

Outside Peter's shanty is a bust of him. The cabin is quite small, three quarters the size of an average English flat, with only three rooms; bedroom, living room and study. Many of Peter's possessions still remain here from his residency, which lasted five years, while he planned and designed Petersburg. When designing grand palaces and his own new city, unlike his descendants, he was never someone who revelled in personal aggrandisement. He lived happily in his sparse log cabin, enjoyed sleeping in the simplicity of his carriage when travelling, and preferred the common man over nobility. This is the part of him most likeable, most content working beside his soldiers and craftsmen, living as they did excelling at creating objects with his own hands Peter also embraced a pronounced love of learning. His major fault was allowing frustration within himself to metamorphose into extreme violence due in part to his bouts of epilepsy, mental illness and childhood trauma.

Across a cobbled courtyard I came to a delightful pavilion, created on the orders of Catherine the Great, to house Peter's boat. Inside is a replica of it, the original dinghy, he learned to sail on the lakes surrounding Moscow, is in the Central Naval Museum. It is a beautiful craft twenty three feet long by six feet seven inches wide, built in 1640 it had belonged to Ivan the Terrible, Peter's grandfather. At the age of sixteen, Peter had found it lying decrepit and rotting in an estate boatyard. This once lovely vessel had been built in England

and given as a gift by Elizabeth 1 to Ivan the Terrible. The Inquisitive Peter asked a Dutch seaman, 'What is the advantage of this type of dinghy?' and was told, 'It is capable of sailing against the wind, unlike Russian boats.' Intrigued Peter asked another Dutch sailor, to restore it.

When repairs were completed, it became the beginning of Peter's naval ambitions. In Russia the boat is known as 'The Grandfather of the Russian Navy'.

From the boat house I walked to a bronze sculpture of Peter, the strangest object, I thought, in the whole fortress. Designed by Mikhail Shemiakin it shows, Peter with small head, modelled from a mask when he was 46 years old and already looking like an old man. By that time he was bald and without the handsome moustache shown in flattering portraits of him. The rest of the statue is exaggerated with an elongated body, spidery fingers and enormous feet. It is a fascinating work of art and one of the most popular sights in the fortress and Petersburg.

Not far from this monument I came across a heavily decorated old man in full naval uniform. Stopping, to say hello, I asked about his medals. He replied he had been a sailor during the Siege of Leningrad (Petersburg) and had become an Admiral. Now he was old he was allowed to earn money, walking the historic fortress, letting tourists take his photo. Months later I sadly realised I hadn't written down his name for my journals.

Leaving the fortress island I next visited the Decembrist Memorial which recalls five officers, of the Imperial Guard, executed in 1825 for attempting to establish a Constitutional Monarchy. The five hundred soldiers, who followed them, were sent to Siberian, hard labour, camps.

The Decembrists, considered Russia's first revolutionaries, are honoured by this obelisk. Since the end of Communism the memorial has sadly become neglected. A poem at the base of it is from Russia's most famous poet, Pushkin.

Dear friend have faith

The wakeful skies presage a wondrous dawn

Russia shall from her age long sleep arise

And despotism shall be crushed

Upon its ruins our names will be incised.

From here I strolled across Birzhevoy Bridge, one of the busiest bridges in Petersburg, with its centre arch that opens to allow large vessels to pass beneath.

One evening I saw this bridge, brightly lit, with its centre open. It was spectacular with lights, defining its shape, glimmering across the water. Other days I noticed it decorated, with bright coloured banners flapping, wildly, in the wind that channels along the Malaya Neva. I found it also a good spot from which to view Petersburg city.

The first palace built in Petersburg was Peter's own Summer Palace, just across the Neva from the Peter and Paul Fortress and with a view of his beloved Log Cabin, so one sunny morning I decided to visit.

Peter's Summer Palace, built 1710-1714, lies on the banks of the Fontanka River. Peter, not given to opulent flamboyancy, used it as his own residence. It is modest in size, looking more like a European Merchants house rather than the palace of Russia's most famous emperor. Peter lived there until his death in 1725. Shining like a block of golden sand, a colour Russians admire no doubt because it reminds them of sunshine, it looks like a two storey office block. It is nothing at all, in any way, like the sumptuous palaces that followed.

Peter the Great.
Founder of Petersburg.

Fontanka River, Petersburg

Cathedral of Spilled Blood.

Grandeur of Russian Cathedrals.

Peter and Paul Fortress.

Tomb of Peter the Great.

Fountains at Peterhof Palace.

Statue at Peterhof Palace.

In the lower floor of this humble residence was Peter's workshop; the upper part he lived in with his wife Catherine and their children.

Peter's wife, Catherine, was one of the most remarkable women in history. Born into a serf family, of Lithuania, her parents dying during a plague, she became an orphan when three years old. A Lutheran Pastor took her into his care and later, when he moved to Latvia, she became his family servant girl. Catherine grew into a teenager of noted beauty. The pastor's wife, jealous of her, married her off, age 17, to a Swedish Dragoon who, after only eight days of happiness, was sent to war and she never saw him again. This beautiful girl was soon reduced to working menially, as a washerwoman for the Russian army and with them was taken to Moscow. There she became, because of her appearance, servant to Field Marshall Sheremetev. Considerably attractive she caught the lustful eyes of Prince Menshikov, a close friend of Peter the Great, and quickly became not only his servant but also his mistress.

One momentous day, when she was twenty years old, Peter saw her and fell in love. She was his lover for eight years before he finally married her. It was a successful relationship that bore them twelve children, ten of whom died.

Catherine is described as energetic, kind, charming and always cheerful and the only person able to calm Peter's frequent rages. On his death, briefly, she became Empress of Russia, the first woman to bear the title. She died aged forty three, two years after Peter, of what is now believed to have been tuberculosis.

So here I was standing at the first palace built in Petersburg and found to my dismay it temporarily closed. I would have liked to see Peter's personal belongings and especially his workshop. Taciturn Marina, accompanying me, suggested we see Peter's Summer Gardens, behind Peter's palace, instead.

The Summer Gardens, begun in 1704 when Peter was beginning his project for his own city, were intended for personal use and that of his friends. They were designed to the style of France's famous Versailles Gardens. To achieve this ambitious plan Peter imported elm and oak trees and commissioned exact copies of celebrated Roman statues, to be set along wide avenues. By 1777 numerous fountains had been added and some 250 statues. Then came a massive flooding of the Neva. It destroyed much of the original carefully planned Garden. At present there are only 89 of the sculptures remaining.

Catherine the Great, calling herself, 'Empress of all the Russias', had this lovely garden redesigned in English style and that's what we see today. At first only nobility were allowed to enjoy this calm space but eventually it opened to Russia's famous and celebrated. Pushkin, Russia's beloved, poet, living nearby, was often seen in the garden writing, sometimes in slippers and robe and feeling so comfortable he referred to it as his home.

On the Neva side the gardens have iron railings, supported by 36 granite columns, such beautifully designed iron gates, with intricately entwined branches and flowers, that visitors from all over Europe come to see them.

With its history of poets, writers and musicians, the Summer Gardens are considered one of the most romantic places in the world. In Imperial Russia whole families would come to show off their sons and daughters, in their most splendid of dresses and attire, with a view to marrying them off.

At one Garden entrance there is an enormous, sixteen feet high, pink porphyry vase presented, to Tsar Nicholas 1 by the King of Sweden in 1839. By then the Gardens were no longer a preserve of nobility and famous but had been opened to army officers and decently attired citizens.

During Petersburg's, corrosive rains of summer the Garden's statues are carefully protected with transparent waterproof covers and in winters by wooden sheaths. The sculptures are remarkably varied; Emperors Claudius and Nero, Cupid and Psyche, sculptures to Truth, Nobility and Beauty, on and on.

Musicians often came to the Gardens; among them were Tchaikovsky and Mussorgsky. You can still, if you are observant, still see Russia's most celebrated and famous strolling down its avenues, drinking coffee in the summer sunshine, or lazing on countless benches under the shade of tall 300 year old trees.

The Garden Coffee House was built in 1826, and since it was a lovely sunny day we sat down there listening to a tall, handsome, man of about thirty playing classical music on a combination xylophone. His playing was so skilful that during a respite, in his repertoire I strolled over to speak with him. He told me, in faultless English, his name was Alexei Chizhik but because he travelled widely in Europe, and England, he sometimes anglicised his name to Chiswick. An accomplished musician Alexei had played in Petersburg's Philharmonic Hall and Mariinsky Theatre.

'I play vibraphone and glockenspiel,' Alexei told me.

Inviting him to a coffee with us I gave him my English address and asked him to visit whenever he was in England. Since meeting him Alexei has formed his own successful Jazz Quartet in which he plays vibraphone.

'I speak several European languages, as well as English, learned while travelling. When I'm not doing concerts I go busking round Europe. In England I can earn £1,400 in one day.'

Marina was undeniably impressed by the handsome Alexei. Noticing this he leaned over to me and whispered, 'Any Russian woman will sleep with you after a glass of wine.' It was said as a matter of fact without smiling.

Marina, overhearing, corrected him, 'Maybe after two.' At which we all laughed.

Leaving the Gardens and the charming Alexei we walked back to Decembrist Square and boarded a river cruise to the Gulf of Finland and mouth of the Neva.

It was pleasantly cool on the river, on such a hot sunny day, and quietly relaxing on the grandeur of the wide Neva.

Beneath the waves river pollution is heavy in the Neva, from hundreds of Petersburg factories pouring virulent waste into its waters. These destructive pollutants are varied, copper, zinc, manganese and sewage join the river. Petersburg's Federal Service has warned that, "No beach along the Neva is safe to swim from". My concern was not swimming but safety of Petersburg's drinking water. I read Petersburg's tap water was safe only after boiling. Everyone, it is suggested, should only drink bottled water. All restaurants and hotels use filtration methods.

We ended the day with dinner in a restaurant near Nevsky Prospect.

Marina told me she needed to take gifts to the Director of the 'Pushkin Flat Museum'. We set off on a dull, cloudy morning to see Pushkin's elegant apartment, facing the Moika Canal.

At this graceful museum we were met by its woman Director, and assistant. They were both delighted to receive the gifts Marina had carefully wrapped, with bows and labelled carefully for them. We were the only visitors, that quiet grey morning, so the Director gave us a personal tour of the celebrated poet's large apartment. It was a typical gentleman's residence of 1830's Petersburg.

Alexander Pushkin, is the most highly revered, and loved poet, in all of

Russia. Two of his works were turned into operas by Tchaikovsky. It was a pleasure for me to learn more about him. The flat is filled with memorabilia from his life, including the couch, he lay dying on after his fatal duel, with his wife's lover, George de Heeckeren d'Anthes. Recently blood, discovered on the couch, has been confirmed, by using DNA, as Pushkin's by comparing it with a lock of his hair also displayed in the museum. The Director showed us the waistcoat Pushkin wore, when he was shot and the bullet hole is there in the garment.

Pushkin had an African ancestor and displayed the same dark curly hair and genetic looks of his distant forbear. Educated at The Imperial Lyceum, where nobles of Petersburg sent their sons, gave him close access to the highest echelons of Petersburg society and though not handsome he was well liked by everyone.

Adultery, acceptable and commonplace in those Petersburg's aristocratic circles, led Pushkin into many duels. Then at 30 years he met, and fell in love with, Natalia Goncharova, an 18 year old, renowned in Petersburg society for her exceptional beauty. She appears to have married him not out of love but to gain access to Petersburg's, flamboyantly excessive, social scene and its notoriously frenzied, frequent, winter balls which were attended by the most powerful noble families in Russia, including Tsar Nicholas 1.

Within six years Natalia had born Pushkin four children and still considered one of the most beautiful women in Russia she attracted the attention of Tsar Nicholas himself, who made blatant overtures to her, dancing with her whenever she attended Petersburg's balls. During the day the Tsar would sometimes ride purposely, beneath her window on horseback, stopping his horse to rear it in an unmistakeably sexual gesture. To make matters worse

Tsar Nicholas disliked Pushkin because of the poet's openly radical, revolutionary ideas. Pushkin was, like many poets, before and since, a visionary dreaming of almost unreachable ideals.

Into Petersburg, at this time, an extremely handsome young Frenchman appeared, the same age as Natalia, named Baron George de Heeckeren d'Anthes, a lieutenant in the Tsar's Horse Guards. This Frenchman had been adopted by Baron Jacob Heeckeren, a homosexual, who had fallen in love with d'Anthes, when a teenager, and they became lovers. A bisexual, George d'Anthes, tall, with blonde wavy hair and blue eyes, looking irresistible in his white and red uniform, fell in love with Natalia. She foolishly encouraged the relationship, in front of all St Petersburg society so, to prevent the ensuing prevalent gossip, d'Anthes hastily married Natalia's sister Ekaterina while still continuing his pursuit of the beautiful Natalia Pushkin. This led to a duel between husband and lover.

Pushkin met d'Anthes early in January 1837, on a cold winter morning, in a snow bound field north of Petersburg. Dishonourably d'Anthes, an experienced soldier, managed to fire first. Pushkin fell to the ground, mortally wounded, with blood spurting from his shattered pelvis. Courageously he struggled to his feet and fired but, in his weakened state, only slightly wounded d'Anthes in the arm. Two days later on 27th January 1837 Pushkin died in this flat, overlooking the Moika, where we now stood. From the position of the wound I wondered was d'Anthes, a soldier experienced with firearms and of unscrupulous character, deliberately aiming to emasculate Pushkin? Personally I think so.

On his death bed Pushkin sent d'Anthes a note saying he forgave him, at which the insolent d'Anthes laughed, derisively, and replied, 'Tell him I forgive him too.' There was no remorse here.

St. Petersburg's elite, until this moment, had little idea how much ordinary Russians felt about their dearly loved poet Pushkin. To everyone's surprise there were angry demonstrations in the streets, calling for the execution of d'Anthes. To appease their anger Tsar Nicholas put d'Anthes, temporarily, in the Peter and Paul fortress, probably to save the Frenchman's life, stripped him of his rank and sent him out of the country. The Tsar vowed to care for Pushkin's family, which he did, paying all of Pushkin's considerable debts and giving Natalia a substantial pension and then made her his mistress, which is what he had always wanted. Six years later Natalia married a soldier, Major General Petr Petrovich Lanskoy to whom she bore three daughters.

Back in France d'Anthes became a successful politician and lived to 84 years. After the death of his wife, Natalia's sister in 1843, d'Anthes once more took up his sexual relationship with Baron Heeckeren his adoptive father.

A moving statue of Pushkin, the vibrant, reckless, courageous poet of Russia looks sadly at visitors to the museum garden.

On leaving this small museum, to Russia's adored poet, the smiling, kindly director gave me two illustrated books, of Pushkin and the museum, as a parting gift.

We strolled along Millionaire's Street, which connects with the narrow, peaceful, tree lined Swan canal leading to Palace Square. Millionaires Street (Millionnaya) is one of the oldest streets in Petersburg, built 1713, and named in memory of the richest family in Russia, the Sheremetev's, who occupied number 19. This street, as its name suggests, is filled with palaces. At number 12 the last Tsar's family often lived, prior to the Revolution, but the oldest building on the street, number 22, belonged to Count Fyodor Apraxin, Russia's first Admiral a lifelong friend of Peter the Greatand renowned for his naval victories, Apraxin owned a palace in Petersburg that was said to be such a noble dwelling that even a king would have been envious. Whoever said that was correct because Apraxin's magnificent palace was demolished to build the Winter Palace on top of it and so all we now have this smaller residence at number 22. Apraxin was buried in Moscow but his grave was deliberately destroyed by Stalin.

This lovely old street leads to New Hermitage where I wanted to see the spectacular Atlantes at the entrance porch. These are giant, grey granite sculptures, eighteen feet in height, set on granite blocks carved by Alexander Terebenev who, working on them for years, with 150 assistants to help him, erected them in 1848. The detail in these sculptures is remarkable even the statues feet display meticulously carved, realistic looking, veins.

Marina, noticing my gaze, said, 'In the summer these toe nails are painted in bright colours.'

One sunny day I visited the Russian Museum, while Marina made one of her frequent visits, with Lara, to see the city administrator. Marina seemed deeply unhappy, and anxious, on these occasions but was non-communicative about her fears.

Catching a metro, to Nevsky Prospect, I ambled Mikhailovsky Street to see the grandly imposing Mikhailovsky Palace. It was one of the most beautiful of Petersburg Palaces, built for the younger brother of Tsar Alexander 1, and converted into 'The Russian State Museum' by Nicholas 11 in 1898. The entrance is across a wide, immaculate, square leading to a Corinthian columned portico, guarded by two white lion sculptures staring coldly, in an eternal warning gaze, at visitors.

The Russian Museum holds the largest collection of Russian art in the world. Any non-Russian visiting it is in for an unforgettable experience. If you aren't aware that Russian artists are among the finest in the world, this museum will enlighten you beyond doubt. Like everything else, in this surprising country, its art is on a grand scale, lavish colour and attention to smallest detail abounds in the compositions. Russian art reflects the emotions and soul of the artist.

I stayed, quite a while, absorbed silently, at the immense grandeur of Karl Briulov's 'Last Days of Pompeii.' This enormous painting which took five years to complete is superb.

Ilya Repin, whose work always catches the breath, is found here also. Everyone's favourite painting of his, I suppose, is his tremendous, sad depiction of 'Barge Haulers on the Volga'. Like many artists and writers of his time, Repin sought to expose the appalling poverty, and inequality, of life in pre-Revolution Russia. It seems unbelievable that Nicholas 11, who admired this painting, was still unable to perceive the awful, chasmic, divide that separated he toil of ordinary Russians from the grand, indolent, lifestyle of the aristocracy.

The Barge haulers depicted in this famous painting were haulers that Repin painted from real life and of men he had grown to admire. The lead hauler, in the painting, was a de-frocked priest named Kanin, described by Repin as, 'A man of dignity, a saint, a colossal mystery'.

Another favourite painting by Repin that most visitors come to see, is the joyfully defiant, 'Reply of the Zaporozhian Cossacks to Sultan Mehemed 1V', that is also based on a true story illustrating Russia's confidence that she will laugh at and conquer all.

The Museum does not include all the finest of Repin's work, some are on display in the magnificent 'Tretyakov Gallery' in Moscow.

A friend of Repin was the artist Victor Vanetsov also on display here. I studied, carefully, his folklore painting 'Knight at the Crossroads', and quickly understood, that though taken from a Russian folktale, it portrays in the weary, battle hardened image of the Knight, the dark, fearful uncertainties facing Russia, in 1878, when it was painted. It is prophetic of the confused sadness of Russian society, during that time, at a crossroad in history and soon to be consumed by the death of old Russia.

Of landscapes painters Isaac Levitan is considered the best but my favourite is Arkhip Kuindzhi whose work conveys a mystical spirituality. One of his paintings aroused an inexplicable sub-conscious recognition in me that I have never forgotten. His painting 'Night Watch' so intrigued me with its beauty, and calm portrayal of dying light, across a sweeping, Dnieper River landscape, that I made a visit to the museum, another day, just to look at it again but found it had been moved to make way for another collection.

The Russia Museum was suffocating on such a hot day so I caught a taxi home. Marina, when I arrived back, was very quiet, tired, laconic and unable to express her feelings so I didn't ask.

One sunny morning we decided to book tickets for the Mariinsky Theatre, still called by some, 'The Kirov'. We set off by tram to endure a long queue waiting to purchase tickets, for a performance of Giselle with principal dancer Alina Samova. In this snail crawl line a twenty year old Russian, noticing my English, commented, 'There is a delay due to a problyema.' Russians, mostly sociable, with many under the age of 50 years, speak some English which they enjoy practicing on western tourists. After speaking to me he shrugged his shoulders in tired acceptance of the delay.

Until this time I had lived with a rosy coloured view of Russia, unable to see below its grand façade to the levels that cause so much dissatisfaction among Russians themselves. In reality I had no idea of the way ordinary Russians lived, or any knowledge of their daily struggles to survive in what has, since the end of Communism, become a 'free for all' society. This blinkered view was about to change with a purchase of tickets, to front stall seats, at the Mariinsky.

Tickets secure in my pocket, we travelled, by trolleybus, down Nevsky Prospect to the Alexander Nevsky Monastery Lavra, at the end of Nevsky's wonderfully wide, thoroughfare.

Lavras are the highest ranked of Russian monasteries and Russia has four them. This one, founded by Peter the Great in 1710, is named after Russia's famous Russian hero, Alexander Nevsky, who defeated the Swedes in 1240. Nevsky had been Prince of Novgorod and, since Peter himself had later also defeated the Swedes, it seemed appropriate to name the Prospect and Monastery after their revered Nevsky.

You may not know but Russians are themselves descended from Swedish Vikings called 'The Rus'.

Nevsky Lavra Monastery is a complex that includes a Seminary for training Orthodox priests and Choir Masters, Trinity Cathedral, Church of the Annunciation and all of it is surrounded by cemeteries.

A broad avenue, crosseing a canal that has two cemeteries either side, leads to the red and white entrance of the Monastery. Above its entrance is a mosaic of the head of Christ. Passed this, Trinity Cathedral, unmistakable with its huge dome, lies just ahead. To the right is a two storey building combining two chapels, one at the top, 'Nevsky Chapel', the oldest, and one below, the 'Church of the Anunciation' built in 1717.

Trinity Cathedral has a remarkable, red and white marble, iconostasis that shows copies of famous religious paintings from around the world. To the right of this a silver reliquary contains Alexander Nevsky's bones. Initially an enormous, silver, sarcophagus held them but this has been moved to the Hermitage. Behind the reliquary is a painting of Nevsky. He was created a saint in the 16th Cent; in Russian Orthodoxy it isn't necessary to be a holy man to become a saint the requirement is that you are greatly esteemed by Mother Russia.

I was truly impressed by this inspiring colourful Cathedral with its old icons and atmosphere of Holiness.

Outside the Cathedral, the Lazarus Cemetery is the oldest in Petersburg, founded by Peter the Great, in 1716, when he buried his sister Natalia Alekseevna there.

Celebrated people, connected with Petersburg, are interred in nearby Tikhvin Cemetery. Here you will see ornate, elegant monuments to composers, Tchaikovsky, Mussorgsky, Glinka, Rimski-Korsakov and writers Dostoevsky and Krylov and in this quiet place can be found tombs of the most famous, artistic and scientific achievers in Russia's clan of genius.

One of the most visited of these tombstones is that of Dostoevsky, with a bust showing his face hardened, by experience and suffering, as any Roman gladiator. On his tomb is an inscription, in Russian, that is a quote from the New Testament Gospel of John.

Often there are beggars at gates of Russian Monasteries so I carried coins to give to them. On this occasion, as we left the Monastery, there was a table from which a man was selling his small cast-aways. Among his intriguing collection I found a metal, glass holder, the kind Russians frequently use for hot drinks. This one had a troika pattern on it.

'Is it old?' I asked in Russian.

'Da, very old,' he replied.

I guessed it was probably from the 1940's and bought it from him hoping Russian Customs would allow me keep it.

We were hot and tired in the close humidity of the day so journeyed home, just in time to miss one of the angry, heavy, hailstorms that often deluge Petersburg during summer.

Petersburg consists of approximately forty two islands, divided into a mosaic of rivers and canals and more than Venice. One clement day, at Festival Square near the Hermitage, I purchased tickets for a canal cruise. The guide on the tour spoke only Russian. This wasn't a problem for me since no one ever remembers what tour guides say anyway. The real delight of the tour was seeing Petersburg's wonderful bridges from the water. There are more than five hundred bridges in Petersburg, crossing its waterways, and many are beautifully spectacular. Palaces, mansions and historic architecture flank these outstanding city canals. I found it relaxingly peaceful viewing these from the small, leisurely moving, canal boat.

After the tour I decided to visit Petersburg's renowned Pushkin's Café.

Near the door, sitting at a round table, quill in hand, a sheet of poetry in front of him as he gazes in contemplation across Nevsky Boulevarde, is an effigy of a not very handsome Pushkin. This is the café he dined in, for the last time before his fatal duel in 1837. On that day he drank only lemonade. We can only guess what he felt, and thought, of his wife's infidelity and the duel ahead. What a difference a day can make when history and lives are changed, by 'Black Swan' events. Russia's most celebrated poet was killed the next day by an immoral rake's bullet.

Pushkins Café is not cheap, dining there needs prior booking but, on this day, a table was free so we sat down to a frugal lunch while listening to classical music played on violin and piano. Downstairs the Café décor is green, designed the way Pushkin would have seen it, but the upstairs dining area, with its red walls and 19th century lighting, I found disconcerting as though it was foretelling the fate that lay ahead for this beautiful city.

It was the 22nd of June a time when the sun refuses to abandon Petersburg and holds back darkness by filling its hours with pearly light so that evening I purchased tickets for the 'White Nights' bus tour. At the ticket booth was another tourist, a voluble, jovial, Italian professor from Rome's Sapienza University, the oldest in Rome.

'I often go to Cambridge in England,' he told me on hearing my English. 'Do you work here?'

'I'm just sightseeing,' I replied.

'Well, the best thing about Russia is the women, incomparable,' he added, charmingly staring into Marina's eyes.

Marina remained unsmilingly silent, in cold distrust.

Russian women adore Italian men; many marry them as their first choice.

'Some cities, I read, have a ratio of five women to every man,' I remarked to the romantic academic.

'And four out of five are beautiful,' he re-joined, then looking once more at Marina said, 'I see we have the same taste in women.'

It was cultural, typical Italian charm, exuded naturally without sincerity.

Our tour lasting five hours beneath a softened glow was worth spending the time, and sleepless night and it was truly very light. Nevsky Prospect was avalanched with people laughing, romancing, drinking coffee and wine enjoying it all.

We watched brightly lit bridges open, over a dazzling ivory coloured, and glistening Neva for cargo vessels to enter port. Palace Bridge, built in 1916, is the most impressive of all. Twenty two bridges, with lights shining across their expanse open twice nightly, between April and September, for shipping. I have never forgotten the sight of these massive, resplendently lit bridges yawning wide, with the Peter and Paul fortress beyond them, similarly brightly lit, imposing across the Neva. From Troitsky Bridge visitors can see seven more Neva Bridges opening.

Once, during Soviet times, an internationally famous Russian pilot, Valery Chkalov, in an attempt to show his girlfriend the ardour of his love for her, and to win her hand, flew madly daringly under Troitsky Bridge. I doubted if any Italian lover would try that.

It had been such a tiringly long day and night Marina flagged down a passing car to take us home. This is common practice throughout Russia and quite legal. Drivers are paid their, always reasonable, asking price and everyone goes home happy. This particular driver knew Petersburg well and got us home far more quickly than any taxi driver I had used around the Nevsky area.

The day came to see the ballet performance of Giselle at the Mariinsky. We Journeyed by tram. I had grown to enjoy Petersburg tram rides, filled with every day working people. Petersburg city trams, slow moving and frequent, are a wonderful way to see the city and its suburbs. From their windows

Petersburg life is on display, with time to observe its smartly dressed businessmen, elegantly dressed women and in contrast, struggling battlers and alcoholics, who in spite of their addiction rarely turn to the mindless violence, arrogance or swaggering, that one sees in Britain and Europe among binge drinkers.

Before the ballet performance we stopped for coffee and light repast in the Mariinsky. This iconic theatre is where, for the first time, I met the endemic corruption and theft engaged in by Russia's government employees and officials.

The Mariinsky has often been in the news, over the years, for its crooked dealings with its celebrated dancers and directors. In 1995 there was a bribery scandal involving millions of dollars transferred to a Swiss bank account by a Mariinsky theatre director and his accomplice the head of choreography. In 2013 a US dancer claimed she had been asked for $10,000 before she would be allowed to dance her solo role. In that same year Artistic Director, Sergei Filin, was injured in an acid attack that left him partially blind.

Valery Gergiev, friend of Vladimir Putin, has been General Director of the Mariinsky since 1988 and one would believe should carry responsibility for all this, happening on his watch, but has never been accused.

On a more mundane level I had paid for tickets in front stalls of the theatre for myself, Marina and Sasha. On arrival we were told our seats were in the third tier balcony, which were much cheaper seats. When Marina questioned this a woman attendant nodded in disgust, at a theatre official, who when we asked her told us that unfortunately there were seats in the theatre with the same numbers in the third tier and there had been a mistake. We had no choice but to accept these while someone pocketed the difference in ticket price and enjoyed our better seats.

From the height of the third balcony we were crushed together, with hardly any knee room, against a balcony front from where the dancers appeared as Lilliputian figures. The performance was mediocre with tired dancers, sluggishly dancing their roles.

The most interesting part of being there was not the performance but seeing the architectural beauty of the theatre itself. A massive amount of funding has been injected into it and disappeared into someone's pocket. The theatre in spite of this funding is still in need of repair even though every performance is filled to capacity and the theatre itself is architecturally beautiful and I was glad to have seen it.

One grey day when Marina had to visit the city administrator, and as always didn't want to talk about it, I began to realise how stressful life in Russia can be for most people.

Alone I went to see one of the largest squares in Petersburg, Sennaya Ploshad. It is said the whole history of Petersburg is reflected in Sennaya Square. Dostoyevsky made it famous in his novel 'Crime and Punishment'. It is an area established, in 1737, to meet the needs of workers who had herded into the growing city. It however accommodated them only poorly and eventually by the 19th century it had become slum, of the squalor and crime, mentioned by Dostoyevsky. Due to its slums, and poverty, Sennaya was the cheapest place to buy produce and so became Petersburg's most popular market. It was also glorified, to give the place hope, with a magnificent baroque church, 'The Church of the Assumption', built in 1753, which the atheist Soviets knocked down to build a metro in 1961.

I arrived at this metro and thought it the most ugly looking station in all of Petersburg.

On the street approaching the metro are bus and marshrutka stations. Marshrutkas are Russia's mini buses the most cheap and convenient form of travel but they are often no more than converted vans with seats unhealthily crammed to capacity.

Sennaya square is extensive, filled with people and cheap foreign imports. Stalls sell fruit, vegetables and unpalatable looking, hard as leather, meat. The square has three metros and is still, as in Dostoyevsky's time, surrounded by one of the poorest suburbs in Petersburg and still rampant with crime.

Walking past a McDonalds fast food I came across a dead woman, on the pavement, lying on her back with stomach badly distended, her head turned to the side and green vomit oozing from her mouth. A small group gathered to stare but most people walked on, without stopping, as though this was a normal occurrence. A policeman glumly stood, forty feet away, doing nothing, waiting for an ambulance.

After this incident I didn't feel like doing much so walked the peaceful, tree lined, Griboedova Canal, close by the square, to see some of its popular, delightful foot bridges.

Later back at my flat I noticed someone had tried to break in. When Marina returned she rang the police who, surprisingly, arrived promptly and took her report. I sat silent in the dining room unable to understand any word said. It was obvious someone had noticed a foreigner living there and had expected to find a lucrative haul. Burglary is rife throughout Russian cities and the reason for those solid, steel clad, doors with numerous safety locks.

Marina, for some reason, was so constantly stressed it made her absent minded. Often on our journeys through the city she lost her way and on metros didn't know which station to use. She had difficulty understanding metro guide leaflets and we often found ourselves travelling all over Petersburg to places we had never intended visiting. One day we spent hours walking the city because she was totally lost. Whenever we stopped to ask directions she then forgot what was said. This disconnection often occurred also when shopping and after I had suggested a list of things I needed she would forget almost immediately. It was apparent to me she was severely, chronically, constantly anxious and afraid, but reluctant to discuss any of it. I was never able to discover its cause but she was nevertheless for all that a pleasant companion, with her elegant beauty, and sometimes creative humour. On good days she was the most knowledgeable guide I could ever have wished for.

The following day, no doubt due to depression, Marina didn't want to get up. Not wishing to impose on her, or Lara, I decided to visit the world famous Peterhof Palace on my own. Unfortunately when I started out, a driving deluge, accompanied by thunder and lightning made such an excursion impractical. I sought shelter in a nearby monastery. After strolling through its dimly lit recesses I offered to make a donation. A nun, selling candles and religious items from her secluded corner shop, refused to accept my money because I wasn't Russian Orthodox. After a moment or two, as I looked at her items for sale, the nun spoke to me in a few brief Russian words I didn't recognise. These holy words allowed the monastery to accept my gift and make it acceptable to the Orthodox faith. It was a pedantic procedure that seemed without common sense or logic but I had already learned Russians are, almost without exception, deeply superstitious and religious.

On such an unpromising day I decided to return home. Why endure being soaked, in the wild and furious storm, sweeping thunderously across streets outside.

By evening, the rain had ceased entirely and the sun came out as though to laugh at everyone. To cheer up the drooping, silent, melancholy Marina I invited her and Lara to a well-known Petersburg restaurant, on the corner of Zagorodny Prospekt where we could enjoy Russian cuisine and a musical evening. The evening evolved into an unforgettable night of excellent food and dancing. Exuberant dancers, in traditional, Russian dress and bonnet, sang enchantingly. Their voices impressed me, as they had in Russia's monasteries and church choirs, with the echoing cadence of Russian voice in song. It's little wonder that several, best-selling, western songs have been blatantly copied from Russian folk music. The intonation of the Russian voice, in song, is ethereally striking in its mellow tone and timbre.

At a table adjacent to ours a Finnish group, of family and friends, were viewing their restaurant bill minutely, one man picking over it like an authoritarian accountant, while his companions were secretly smirking at him. I noticed them because Finns are genetically good looking people.

Later, when the restaurant had cleared tables for dancing, on the dance floor a handsome Italian man, who had found a tall, beautiful Russian female was doing his best to keep up with her.

We arrived home late. Marina, no doubt missing her husband, was still in deep depression. She wanted to sleep all through the following day but finally rose from her bed, at eleven thirty am. Then the unexpected happened all water to our flat stopped flowing and it was already too late, once more, for me to visit Peterhof.

Deciding it was time to absent myself, for a while, to give my guides a break, I contacted the Dean of Yaroslavl University, whom I had met on my flight when journeying to Samara.

'Is it convenient for me to visit you and your family in Yaroslavl,' I asked.

'Yes, of course, you are always welcome. My parents are at their Dacha. You can stay in their flat if you wish. I am sure they will be happy for you to visit'.

Marina accompanied me to a ticket kiosk at Moskovsky Railway Station, from where the train departs for Yaroslavl, but once more she got lost. This time it took us hours to find the Station.

The Moskovsky Station, an impressive, enormous, building across a wide square was built between 1844-1851 during the reign of Tsar Nicholas I. Inside the Station is a statue of Peter the Great looking very much like a Roman general. The hall surrounding it is encircled by shops and cafes in which to endure the long waits that Russians have endured forever as a part of daily life.

We queued one hour to obtain a ticket so slow were the assistants at the ticket booth checking every passenger's internal and international passports. Then we were told it would probably be three more hours before we could be given a ticket, while they conducted searches, but consoled us by adding if we rang them instead of waiting, a ticket could be delivered the next day.

At my flat, the water supply still wasn't running. I asked a neighbour in an adjoining apartment if their water had stopped also.

'No everything is alright,' I was told.

At the ground floor grocery shop they too said there were no problems at all with their water supply or plumbing.

Marina suggested I try to obtain a rail ticket, to Yaroslavl, from an alternative rail station. Such unnecessary confusion is an everyday occurrence in Russia. I came across it too frequently.

Once more we set off to another railway station only to find it no longer in use. Now we needed to go to Baltiysky Rail Station instead.

Baltiysky Station is another architectural delight, built between 1854 and 1857, at a time when Russia was striving to modernise and equalise a pace with Europe. Here too was a spacious ticket hall surrounded by shops.

I was becoming used to what seemed to be deliberate delays, caused by a lumbering, incomprehensible bureaucracy. At this station a ticket clerk took one hour to handle five people. When it came to my turn I was told I could only have a ticket to Yaroslavl on even numbered days and then only one way. I could only leave on a Sunday not the Saturday I had asked for.

In total we had spent around eight hours trying to buy a railway ticket. If it hadn't been for the energetic antics and humour of Marina's daughter Lara I would have been wholly despondent. This inexplicably comic way of life, for average Russians, is imposed without any resemblance of logical order. Eventually, worn down by these wilfully engineered delays, I suddenly found it as amusing, as mischievous Lara, and the three of us returned home laughing.

Next day there was still no water connected to our flat. Marina tried ringing local government plumbers. There was no reply on any of their department numbers. We had no choice but to visit their offices personally.

Perplexed we walked through monotonously dull grey streets, all looking alike in drab Soviet uniformity, but we couldn't locate the government offices. Eventually, after three addresses and enquiring several times from local residents, we found a government office hidden without even a sign to show it was there, across a wide court-yard. The next obstacle was finding an attendant to discuss our lack of running water. Inside the building was a queue of disgruntled Russians waiting in a corridor. One old, tired woman told us the attending clerk hadn't shown up for work.

In this shabby, brown and cream walled, hall several frustrated people were waiting beside the plumbing manager's door. They knew he was in there, a cord from a cleaners vacuum ran from a plug, in the corridor, right underneath the managers locked door.

Puzzled by this I asked an exasperated elderly Russian woman, standing glumly and totally lost, what was wrong.

'He is in there having sex with the cleaning lady, that's why the door is locked,' she answered angrily.

An athletic looking man walked into the corridor in a violent anger and forcefully tried to get into the manager's office. Unable to break it open he walked away, a grim scowl scarring his face. Shortly after he came back again and tried to batter down the door with his shoulder and boots.

Another cleaning lady entered the corridor to tell us she couldn't clean any of the offices because someone had broken an electric wire that connected the electric sockets to each other.

Overhearing the noise and arguing in the corridors, an adjoining office door was suddenly opened by a robust woman, with fists like sledge hammers, to fiercely tell us, 'The plumber is on holiday for three weeks.'

No one believed her.

I turned to Marina and as politely as I could asked, 'Can you kindly find me a different flat and ask for my money back for the one I am in?'

'Yes but I have to get all documentation together, and a phone number, from my friend Tatiana.' Marina replied, with unreadable poker face. She didn't appear at all concerned about lack of progress in resolving our plumbing problems. To her it was normal life in Russia.

Back at our flat the phone rang and a man on the line told us a plumber would be over to see us by 2.00 pm. After our experiences I thought this most unlikely.

When time came for the plumber to arrive, dark clouds had appeared off the Baltic Ocean. For thirty minutes a vertical downpour was accompanied by thunder. These sudden storms are frequent in Petersburg, during summer, and after their angry outburst skies clear, as quickly as they had darkened. Petersburg evenings however are invariably delightfully cool and sunny.

At around 4.30 pm a plumber rang to say he would be able to fix our water supply between 9-10 am the next day. I doubted this also. It had been another wasted day for us. I began to realise, every day is one of continuous frustration, for average people in Russia unless you have wealth enough to bribe someone.

Evening came; Marina and Lara went to visit friends for about four hours. I spent my time writing cards to friends around the world. During the day I had purchased litres of bottled water for normal use, drinking and ablutions. I longed to shower but that was impossible in my waterless apartment.

As we knew would happen, the expected plumber still didn't show up the following morning. At 10.20 am I suggested we go to Tsarskoe Selo the Palace where Nicholas 11 spent most of his time avoiding the stress of crisis enveloping his empire. Marina thought I would enjoy travelling by Marshrutka, the Russian minibus method of transport and it is a superb way of meeting everyday working Russians, who are naturally sociable people and far more so than any other country I have travelled in.

Tsarskoe Selo, where Tsar Nicholas 11 preferred to live, is a Summer Palace, sixteen miles to the south of Petersburg, set in timbered countryside.

Peter the Great's wife Catherine had owned the estate and in 1708 built a country house and garden there as a surprise for her husband. Originally the estate had been known as 'The High Place' but its name was changed to Tsarskoe Selo, the Tsar's Village, after Peter's death. Peter's beloved daughter Elizabeth inherited the estate from her father and in 1749 began a total reconstruction of it under the direction of Russia's most famous architect of the time Francesco Rastrelli who had designed the splendid Winter Palace.

No one built palaces like Russians; Tsarskoe Selo, with a frontage of 978 feet in blue and white, is surrounded by classic sculptures. Its gardens are a treasure of long avenues of trees, lake, canal, pavilions and graceful bridges.

A man climbed aboard the overcrowded Marshrutka we on and took a fancy to Marina, from the moment he saw her, and asked her, suggestively, to sit on his knee, at which the other passengers smiled. This behaviour is quite normal among Russian men. Marina rebuffed him with one of her icy, threatening stares.

We exited, at the small town of Pushkin, to walk to a famous sculpture of the poet after whom the town is named. Of all the depictions of Pushkin I have seen this one is surely the best. It shows him sitting on a bench, head resting on his right hand, as he gazes contemplatively into the distance. His life of struggle, romance and poetry, betrayal and fatality, is displayed in this effigy like a microcosm of Russia itself.

From here a walk leads to 'The Lyceum', adjoining Tsarskoe Selo Palace. Pushkin had studied there and been one of its most brilliant of students and here at age 14 he had first recited some of his poems. Tsar Alexander 1 founded the Lyceum in 1811 to educate sons of prominent families to equip them for Imperial Service.

Tsarskoe Selo, where Nicholas 11 and family spent most of their time, also became the place they were confined after the Revolution and on its grounds they were forced to do manually labour.

The whole of the Palace is a stupendous sight but in need of much repair after decades of Soviet neglect. In some parts it looks forgotten. So many people were queuing at the entrance I decided not to join them and instead walk through its lovely Catherine Gardens.

Later, on our return, to the Palace, an old female attendant showed us the renowned Agate and Jasper Rooms, pointing out bullet holes made by destructive German soldiers firing randomly, at the famous amber walls, during World War 11. She proudly led us to the original, masterfully created, parquetry floors, dating from the time of Catherine the Great, still shiny, polished and preserved.

Inside Catherine's Palace you quickly notice Catherine's obsession with sex. Rooms are filled with erotica, consciously intended, to arouse her guests, and encourage flirtation and intimacy.

Away from Petersburg the change in quality of air at Pushkin village was noticeable and invigorating. Allergies, I had endured in Petersburg just disappeared in the breeze of Russia's countryside.

Tired, after such a busy day, and back at the flat I boiled enough water, from our slowly trickling faucets, for Marina to bathe in but I had to be satisfied with a cold wash down. Afterwards we took a leisurely stroll round the district nearby.

Petersburg, like Moscow, is a city of wide contrast. Youths, expensively attired, carrying mobile phones, tablets and driving flashy cars mingle side by side with people struggling to exist.

A pack of four wild dogs slunk down the pavement, opposite to us, ignoring everyone in their determined direction. Seeing my surprise Marina explained, 'They are quite common and well known in Peters. They make me afraid whenever I see them. Once I saw a pack of twelve.'

These feral dogs look like small Alsatians, or American coyotes, and I wondered if they were urban wolves, but no they are just wild dogs, known for frequenting Petersburg's metro stations where they calmly use metros to travel between suburbs in search of food.

Back home once more I realised we could wait for ever for local authority plumbers so I decided to fix the plumbing problem myself, if possible. With tools found in the kitchen drawers, a screwdriver and an adjustable spanner, I traced where the water pipes entered the apartment and discovered, hidden behind a toilet screen blind, there was a valve connecting our water supply to an outside source. With as much energy as I could rally I turned the stubborn valve, to its full extent. It suddenly freed whatever was blocking the pipes and restricting water pressure. Now we enjoyed a far superior flow of water than when I first came there and with it came hot water also.

Marina congratulating me, smiling, said, 'A man has a man's mind and a woman has hers.'

Later that evening a phone call, disturbing our latesupper, came from the government plumber's office. A man, asked, 'Did the work we undertook on your plumbing resolve the problem?'

Marina told him no one had been at all. The man seemed surprised and abruptly hung up when she explained we had fixed it ourselves. No doubt they would in their records state they had completed the work satisfactorily.

'Marina,' I joked, 'you should have told him it was a pity he didn't come because I was going to give the plumber a $100 tip.' We laughed at the thought it would have frosted him over.

Saturday came, warm, sunny. We set off happily, for Peterhof, by bus and ferry, on which I was charged, as a foreigner, almost double the price Russians paid, and we were given the poorest seats. In spite of that it was an enjoyable sixteen mile journey along the southern shore of the Gulf of Finland.

The Palace of Peterhof is the number one tourist attraction outside of Petersburg, and the summer thronged with tourists. This enchanting place, founded by Peter in 1705, is like no other Palace on Earth. It was built, on natural terraced prominences, overlooking the Gulf of Finland. With his lifelong love of ships, and the sea, Peter always preferred to be near open water with its added promise of rapid escape.

A delightful feature of Peterhof is its Gardens. Two cascades of fountains, tumble, like shining crystal, down steep staircases. One, known as 'The Great Cascade', falls in steps to a pool, in the centre of which stands a golden statue of Samson tearing apart the jaws of a lion from which, in its frozen agony, a perfect rod of water shoots skywards to the height of eighty feet. This majestic statue, placed here in 1821, was stolen by looting Germans during World War 11. The one we see now is an exact replica, sculptured in the 1940's.

There are five fountains in the Gardens and its upper and lower parks. After walking through these lovely parks I wished I could have seen them in the rosy, leaf falling, days of autumn or in the silence of winter snows.

The Great Palace of Peterhof was the favourite residence of Peter. It glows, joyously, brightly yellow, with white topped, gilded domes but sadly many of its interior treasures were plundered by Nazi soldiers.

The architect, of this stately Palace, was Jean Baptiste Alexandre le Blond who had been taught by celebrated architect of the time, named Le Notre, who had designed the gardens of Versailles. Peter liked le Blond, about whom he once commented, 'He is better than the best,' to which Le Blond in turn replied, 'Peterhof is Versailles by the sea.'

It is more than a beautiful Palace estate; it is a display of the grandeur, and power, of Peter's Russia, a proud show case of Russia's wealth to the monarchs of Europe. Peter's personality however was nothing like that of the French monarchs, who revelled and debauched, at Versailles. In the gardens of Peterhof is a, one storey, smaller palace, named 'Monplaisir', that Peter preferred even more than his ostentatious Great Palace. Here was his study where, from large windows, he could look over the sea to the Gulf of Finland.

Though Peter built stupendous palaces, for the world to admire, for himself he preferred to live in small, personalised spaces.He hated walled cities where there was no way of escape. I believe views of the sea gave Peter a chance to dream, beyond the range of most men and, like many great men, think all things were possible and his enormous capacity for work and study made it all come true.

Peter was not unsociable and at times excessively indulged himself. At Monplaisir he often invited dignitaries, and close friends, to meet him for drinking bouts that began at breakfast. By evening everyone was drunk. His closest friends were, like his wife, people of humble beginnings who had become renowned achievers. During all his carousing, and in contrast to European monarchs, he was not promiscuous. Apart from his wife, and beloved daughter Elizabeth, he had no other family ties or relationships.

Peterhof Gardens extend to 1500 acres of manicured, natural scenery. In the 19th century fetes were held here, in the month of July, when all of

Petersburg was urged to come and join in. During summer months a military band filled the gardens with music daily and three times a week the Imperial Court Orchestra gave free concerts.

For these stupendous Gardens Peter ordered tens of thousands of trees to be brought from Europe, limes, maples, fruit trees and chestnuts. Over the years the gardens grew into a verdant enchantment. When World War 11 came the Germans, who occupied Peterhof from 1941 to 1943, cut down 14,000 of these two hundred year old trees and mindlessly took pleasure in uncontrolled, vandalism of fountains, dams and statues, as well as theft of that wondrous statue of Samson and the lion and a statue of Peter. What happened to them afterwards I couldn't discover, they were lost or destroyed.

Russians, are justly proud of their history, and as early as 1944, after every German soldier had departed in humiliation, began to restore their beloved Peterhof and its gardens. Tens of thousands of residents, from Petersburg and surrounding areas, gave their weekends free to help with the restoration. The lost statue of Samson and the Lion and the statue of Peter were reconstructed by using details from drawings and photographs. It speaks undeniably of Russian defiance, their national sense of identity, and unconquerable spirit. With this remarkable restoration came a new name, for the Palace and Gardens, 'Petrodvorets', meaning Peters Palace, but ordinary Russians ignored this and still call it Peterhof, as they did from the beginning and so do now.

Something is always happening to capture your attention when visiting this most unforgettable place. Screaming, laughing, children run across stones, of two fountains, to spontaneously trigger jets of water when their feet touch them. This had been a comic idea of Peter's to play tricks on his most aristocratic visitors.

In spite of crowds, and constant activity, Peterhof conveyed a sense of peace, and continuity, that I was reluctant to leave. Back at the ferry quay a man, with a tame Russian bear, was lucratively allowing tourists to stand beside it for photos.

In the evening Marina seemed quite ill again so we stayed home. She made Russia's well-known Borsch soup for us instead. This favourite, of all Slavic people, is basically cabbage with added onions, tomatoes, potatoes, carrots, beetroot, garlic and sour cream and is healthy and non-fattening.

Sunday came and I made my way to the train station to catch the 5.20 pm to Yaroslavl. Instructions were very precise, train number 45, platform 5, carriage 16, compartment 6, and seat 11. I had reserved a sleeper for the 377 miles journey. Because we had arrived early, with time to spare, we walked around Chkalovska, before catching a final metro to the train station.

Chkalovska is a pleasant place to stroll. We found time to eat in a charming restaurant, that was inexpensive, with pretty, neatly attired, waitresses who served us meat filled pancakes.

The entrance to the Chkalovska Metro displays a sculpture of a rugged looking aviator, Valery Chkalov, after whom the metro is named and the whole station has an aviation theme.

The Yaroslavl train was waiting silently when we arrived. Russian trains have enviable double sleeper compartments, with the one disadvantage that if you are travelling alone, you never know who will share the cabin with you.

Marina dressed elegantly, in cream coloured suit, to see me off; made sure I got into the correct carriage and right compartment. Leaving ones friends is never enjoyable. I was sorry to say goodbye to her and Lara.

Settling into the carriage, waiting for the train to depart, I thought of my experience of Russia so far, thinking how resilient Russians are, the way they take everything in their stride, with unmoved fatalism, ignoring hard lives, mafia crimes, government corruption, marital breakdowns, and forever waiting stoically on freezing railway stations and enduring the incurable incompetence of Russian officials. It is a land, and people, impossible to understand or forget, as enduring as time itself.

5.20 TO YAROSLAVL

The compartment I was shown to had carpeted floor, two large mirrors, six wall lights, a locker beneath my bed, a breakfast table beneath the window, two pillows, windows had two sets of curtains for privacy a television, a locker space for extra bags and wardrobe with coat hanger hooks. The cabin was air conditioned, the door could be locked, there were face towels and extra blankets and everything spotlessly clean, even the outside windows. A carriage attendant could be called at any time by pressing a button.

Before the train departed a professional looking man of about sixty, with thick head of white hair and well-dressed, entered my compartment. He would be my companion for the next 377 miles.

Beyond the city limits evening became coolly sunny. We passed through a Russian landscape of birch forests and pine. Our train crept slowly, hypnotically sounding the tracks, as it passed beside small dacha communities and distant lonely farms. There were forests one could hide in forever. Vistas of enormous, flat, interminable spaces fled by our window. Wild flowers bloomed, white, blue and mauve, beside the rail tracks and carpeted the fields with colour. Forest trees danced their leaves in the fading light beneath skies as wide as the eternal landscape and filled our view with dreamy, cumulus clouds soaring in the distance.

After one and half hours the train stopped in the middle of nowhere. I would have liked to get out to enjoy the open air, and wild scenery, on such a lovely evening but couldn't. After twenty five minutes the train began its journey again. Russian trains are known for perfect timing and this break was to pace the train's speed. We continued passed charming wooden villages, scattered over the hills of a valley dissected by a broad lazy river sliding through and farther along I noticed logging communities.

The train stopped at Bologoe, a small town on the edge of a large lake. Here my carriage companion, who had remained silent, invited another man, from a cheaper carriage, to join us. Fortunately this man spoke English and told me he was a musician and my travelling companion a well-known Russian orchestral conductor who performed all over the world. They were on their way to give a concert in Yaroslavl. They sat side by side talking while eating pickles, dried fish and raw sausage, a meal Russians enjoy, which I thought unpalatable. My regret is not writing down the names of this popular conductor and his musician friend.

My sleeper bed was comfortable. I slept soundly until 4.00 am then rose to clean my teeth and shave. My companion was already up and smartly dressed. Through the carriage window a spectacular golden sunrise filled our compartment with light as we passed more wooden villages. A ground mist was rising from the fields like a forgotten cloud. Contemplation, of this peaceful scene, was interrupted by an attendant bringing us coffee at 5.00 am sharp. The train was on perfect schedule.

Exactly at 5.30 am the train stopped at Yaroslavl where Svetlana, in bright blue jacket, with Kate her daughter, was there to meet me.

'Thank you both for coming at such an early hour,' I greeted.

'We came from my parent's dacha and had to get up at 4.00 am.' Sveta laughed taking my arm, 'I will have to leave you with Kate for the day because I have to leave for University at 7.00.'

Yaroslavl, an important railway hub, is also a stopping place for the Trans-

Siberian Railway, one of the longest and most celebrated train rides in the world. Gazing around I found the platform, monotonously long without anything to break its utilitarian dullness.

Sveta in her German Opel, drove through a large square, near her home, to accustom me to the surroundings before going to her parents flat where I would be staying. Her father had been a Soviet factory director. Their flat, one of the finest in Yaroslavl, was on a historic street where, before the Revolution, wealthy merchants and the elite of the city had lived. In Soviet times Party members, and professionals, had been given these privileged residences. It was luxurious with three spacious bedrooms, a kitchen diner and large living room.

Leading me to the second floor Sveta informed me, 'My parents are away at their dacha, as I mentioned, and you are very welcome to stay here. We will go and meet them when I find time.' Smiling, hugging me, she added, 'Kate will show you around while I'm at lectures.'

An academic, Dr Svetlana taught in the History Faculty of Yaroslavl University. The University had been built in 1803, as a Lyceum, a place of higher education for the nobility but over the years it had grown in size and had become recognised for its excellence and popularity. This all ended, in 1918, when Communist rioters set fire to it. Much of the Lyceum went up in the conflagration and most of it had to be demolished. It was not opened again until 1970 and given the status of University. Since then it has continued to expand and now has nine faculties.

Before leaving Sveta, showing me into a large bedroom, said, 'Settle in, I have to leave now. Kate will help you.'

One of the oldest and famous cities on the Volga River, Yaroslavl began life as a Viking trading post. Prince Yaroslav the Wise, Prince of Rostov, a descendant of the marauding, Viking Rus, established a centre here.

Kate, not yet in her teens, slept till 10 am. After breakfast we set off to see this famouscity. I noticed immediately the air was clean pollution free and the city quietly calm and peaceful everywhere. Its street plan hadn't changed from the medieval days in which it had become so prosperous. Peter the Great, revering Russian history, liked to be in places that gave a sense of tranquillity and he often visited Yaroslavl preferring it over the disquiet and unpredictable violence of Moscow.

Our first pause was to see where the city's founder, Prince Yaroslav the Wise, had legendarily, single-handedly, killed a bear with his axe near the banks of the Volga. Yaroslav had wanted free passage on this section of the river, but local bandits, confronting him, set a she bear against him. He courageously dispatched the bear and struck terror in the hearts of the pirate community of the region. Prince Yaroslav stayed and created an administrative centre and fort that has lasted for nine hundred years. He went on to become the Grand Prince of Kiev.

This historic site, at the conjunction of Volga and Kotorosl rivers, has been turned into an exhaustingly long park on the promontory river intersection. Fountains, a monument, and elegant street lamps lead the way. It is beautiful, on a sunny day, but you find it a most miserable, exposed place, when rain and wind howl or snow storms along the rivers. Kate said very little about it and was sceptical about the site. Later she took me to a green sward, nothing like the modern park we had just seen, to show me an untidy, overgrown hollow.

'This is the real place where Prince Yaroslav killed the bear,' she told me confidently. There was nothing to see here, no marker or memorial, but local folklore said this was really where it had happened not on that stylised, touristy, romantic park.

In any case the event gave this, UNESCO city, its Yaroslavl flag of a Russian bear carrying a Viking battle axe. The wise, determined Viking, Prince Yaroslav, successfully made this location, on two rivers, his trading base.

Kate was only twelve and seemed deeply unhappy. It was a large task for a girl of her age to act as guide to a foreigner. I only agreed she do this to please her mother. I just listened and tried to be as kindly as I could.

Sveta, Kate's mother, married early and had divorced soon after the death of her second child, a boy, had died. Her talented husband now lived in America. Like all young girls Kate missed having a father near. We walked silently beside the banks of the Volga River. Though Katya's English was excellent it failed her when we entered a restaurant. I tried to buy dinner for us but she had no idea what Russian dishes were in English, or pretended not to. I believe she was just reluctant to have me spend money on her. I hadn't brought a dictionary with me so we just drank coffee.

It was a stifling warm day. After coffee, noticing a street vender selling the ubiquitous, Russian weak beer, Kvas, I stopped to buy a glass at which Kate, who disapproved of alcohol, gave me a piercing, disapproving glance but I enjoyed it anyway and the we visited Yaroslavl Museum to see its remarkable art and icon collection.

Russian paintings are mostly ignored in the West but I began to see them as more beautiful than any Dutch or Italian works I had seen in any of the world's galleries. There is an intimate spiritual awareness present in Russian art that is rarely found in any other country. Yaroslav Museum's icons had been rescued from Churches destroyed by Soviets.

Kate enthused, 'They are rare and very important.'

For her, like most Russians, they were not just art but objects of reverence. She had been brought up to understand icons draw you into a subconscious reality of God's holiness and presence.

The oldest icon in the Museum is a 13th century Christ Pantocrater (Ruler of All). I hadn't acquired Kate's knowledge or reverence for icons, at this stage, but wondered at their symbolism and age, and the presence of the artist from those ancient days.

From the Museum we walked beside Churches, three hundred years old or more, defunct, locked, dismally sad, and neglected, like some abandoned lover. They weren't always like that.

Baron August von Haxthausen, a German polymath, came to Yaroslavl in 1845 and wrote of seeing 200 church spires and domes in a city that had only 25,000 inhabitants. Theophile Gautier, another 19th cent traveller, described Yaroslavl as the most prestigious of ancient, cultural and religious of Russian cities.

Many of Yaroslavl churches had been paid for by wealthy merchants. Since its foundation, the city had been a major trading centre. In 1553 Richard Chancellor, an English explorer, came here to create a trading base for English merchants to sell wool to the Russians. Chancellor was much impressed by the rich soil and corn that Yaroslavl was able to send to Moscow, "700 to 800 sledges," he wrote. English merchants came here, in an agreement with Ivan the Terrible, and from it traded as far as Persia and India.

Russian Princes preferred Yaroslavl's Monasteries above all others. By the 17th century merchant traders began commissioning splendid churches, elaborately filled with icons and colourful frescoes. A motto of the people of

Yaroslavl, discovered on a church bell, stated, not the Biblical quote "Love conquers all" but "Labour conquers all."

Carl Lebren, an artist from Holland, visiting Yaroslavl in 1702 to paint a panorama of the city wrote of it, "…it can be mentioned among the best of Russian towns. Many rich merchants live here."

Communism came with State Atheism, and 80% of Yaroslavl's enchanting, sacred, churches were destroyed. After this ignorant vandalism only 43 remained standing. Valuable icons, crosses, silver and gold cups were stolen by the Soviets but devout Yaroslavans hid much of their sacred art, and treasures, for safety and a future they believed would come. Some of these are now preserved and displayed in this Museum.

Soviet hatred of the Russian Church was not entirely without reason. Through centuries of serfdom Church hierarchy had remained silent and in many ways enslaved the people as much as the nobility.

Arriving home, Kate shyly retiring to her private room left me alone at the dinner table.

Nights were still bright and summer days long. Sveta drove us, that evening, into the countryside to visit their family graves. It was her way of welcoming me into her family. She showed me her grandfather's grave, a man she had loved a great deal, and sadly nearby the grave of her son, who had died after a few weeks of life. This memory disturbed her so much that on the way home I noticed her crying silently. The loss of a child, the break-up of one's marriage, that's hard to carry. To take her mind off it we went bowling and, for the privilege, were charged twice the price you would pay in England.

The next day Kate still didn't seem well so I let her sleep and set off alone for Yaroslavl's, Volga River, and wharf.

An enormous, Volga cruise, ship was preparing for its 2000 miles journey to the Caspian Sea. These cruise ships are jointly owned, with European companies, and can carry approximately 250 passengers. They aren't considered the best, generally having poor food and cabin facilities. The cruiser, I stood beside, was due to embark at 1.30 pm. I would have liked to observe its departure but not wanting to wait, several hours, I set off to see one of Russia's most original Museums, 'The Museum of Music and Time'.

This museum, owned by John Mostoslavsky, a professional magician and illusionist, is the most remarkable, and unusual, museum I ever visited. Mostoslavsky for years had been fascinated by antique clocks and musical instruments and began collecting and storing them in his, early 19th century, merchant house. It eventually became this Museum of Music and Time. The collection has grown into a wonderland of not only clocks and musical instruments but also of old samovars, flat irons, hand bells and phonographs. Every available space on floor, wall and shelf is filled to capacity. What began as a museum of music and time became a museum of music and every day Russian family items throughout time. This museum has a dreamlike, fairy tale, atmosphere completely in accord with the illusionist's mind that created it.

Returning home I noticed Kate deeply depressed. I suggested she return to bed and sleep. Our flat was hot, on this sultry summer afternoon, without any flow of air entering its small open windows.

Later, full of energy, Sveta returned home to drive us 60 miles to her parent's country dacha. The dacha complex was an untidy landscape with little room for a vehicle to drive along its narrow, dirt roads. Their dacha, was nothing like the two storey one, I had visited in Samara.

Sveta's father had been director of a large Soviet chemical plant. In Soviet times directors were chosen by factory workers and had to be well liked as well as competent. Yuri was certainly likeable with his calm, kindly disposition. We immediately took to each other, as he welcomed us into their delightful, economically furnished, wood cabin. He had severe breathing problems, no doubt brought on by the notoriously unhealthy Soviet chemical industry he had worked in. In childhood he had endured, and survived, the sufferings of the most devastating siege, ever known, when the Nazis surrounded and cut off Leningrad (Petersburg) from the rest of the world. This act of gigantic cruelty had been one of the most brutal offences of Hitler's Third Reich and I find it incredible that Russia was ever able to forgive them. The awful siege, lasting fifteen months, caused the deaths of one and a half million citizens, the greatest loss of life, ever recorded for one city, throughout all of history. The formidably determined Russians nevertheless managed to evacuate one million women, and four hundred thousand children, from this devastation historians have called an act of genocide. Yuri had been evacuated over the truly remarkable 'Ice Road' of Lake Ladoga.

Sveta's mother, Klaudia, strong, silent and reserved, greeted me warmly but with critical gaze, perhaps wondering what I was doing with her supremely successful and beautiful daughter.

Over coffee Yuri suggested we have an evening barbecue at their brick lined barbecue pit. I started to light a fire but noticing evening was closing in rapidly and an ominous, cloudy red, sky tinting the horizon beyond the trees I suggested we abandoned this idea and everyone agreed.

At the end of the dacha garden a confined, muddy, river ran gently between rows of birch trees and wild fruit bushes. Sveta came out to the garden in a, one piece swim suit and asked me, 'Would you like to swim.' I refused politely, suspecting much of the dacha complex waste ended up in this sluggish river. Undaunted Sveta dived in, she had done this since childhood, and swam out of sight for what seemed ages, while Klaudia, more comfortable with me, poured out a glass of red wine as we sat in an adjoining, wood roofed, summer shelter.

When we left, Yuri thrust a three feet high wood carved Russian bear, the symbol of Yaroslavl, into my hands. I accepted the gift gracefully, knowing full well I couldn't possibly carry it back to England, or on any of my journeys. He also presented me with old photos of Yaroslavl and Sveta too gave me gifts. I was touched by their kindly generosity.

Sveta's salary, sometimes not paid at all by the education system, was small, Yuri and Klaudia's pension inadequate. One trial of life in Russia, due to corruption in local and national authority, for Government employees, including the military, is having to wait months before salaries are paid even though they are supposed to be paid monthly. Once a Russian travel agent, offering parents a chance to send their children to overseas camping holidays, told me that often local administrators never make up the accumulating deficits, of salaries, due to endemic corruption, of politicians, at all levels.

One morning, waking with a painfully sore throat, I had difficulty swallowing. I had been awake, most of the night due to severe stomach pain that nothing seemed to relieve. On this day I wanted to stay in bed but Kate, whom I didn't want to disappoint, suggested we visit Spassky Preobrazensky Monastery. Even worse she wanted us to climb the tortuous steps, designed to give anyone a heart attack, to its famous bell tower. Aware my time in Yaroslavl was limited, and I may never return, I acquiesced, shook off the pain and off we set.

Spassky Monastery, the oldest building in Yaroslavl, founded in the twelfth century at the junction of the Kotorosl and Volga Rivers, is now a museum reserve surrounded by a massive, hundred years old, defensive wall. It appears more like a fortress than a place of worship. The original, eight hundred year old, church was destroyed by fire in 1501 but due to its religious importance was immediately rebuilt, a task that took ten years to accomplish.

Foreigners, especially English merchants, carried on business in the ports of Yaroslavl. The historic, defensive walled, monastery was often a safe haven for them in times of trouble.

When Polish and Lithuanian princes invaded Russia, in a war that lasted thirteen years, Spassky Monastery, like a Kremlin behind its fortified walls, allowed the citizens of Yaroslavl to successfully repel these ravaging invaders and send them back to Moscow.

The Monastery has one of the best museums in all of Russia holding approximately 300,000 items in its collection including, one of the oldest manuscripts in Russian, a poem named 'The Tale of Igor's Campaign,' written in the twelfth century. The museum also displays the oldest of Russia's paintings and traditional crafts and rare hand written books and exhibits a priceless collection of icons, from the 15th to 18th centuries. There is too a natural history display of the Yaroslav region.

Beneath the monastery lies a tunnel, leading to rooms that store more collections and surprisingly alongside former prison dungeons.

We walked the monastery's wide walls before climbing exhausting steps to the top of the bell tower. From here are panoramic views of the Kotorosol and Volga rivers, Yaroslavl City and the hills beyond. The bell tower had also been watch tower from which invading armies could be observed and its bells rung to warn Yaroslavl citizens, and traders, to come to safety within the powerful walls of the monastery.

There was a caged, friendly, Russian bear, kept at the museum as symbol of the city. We stood beside it, having our photographs taken by its keeper who then unexpectedly wrote a message in my guide book.

Russian bears, about which I knew nothing until this meeting, are often named Mishka. They frequently feature, in Slavic mythology, as exceptional wise. With one of the largest brains of any animals they are highly intelligent, and perceptive, and have been observed using tools to obtain food. In the wild Russian bears can live to 25 years but in captivity between 40 and 50 years. They are not dangerous to humans, unless feeling threatened, and in places where they are most numerous, an average of only ten people, per annum, die from confrontation with them.

The bear we saw, called Masha, was large, white faced and playful and enjoyed the company of visitors. It had been at the monastery for ten years, after been orphaned when hunters had killed her mother. During summer months, the bear loved bathing and in winter retired to hibernate, in her hay filled den, until March the following year.

Sveta came home late at 6.30 pm, very tired, looking exhausted, but still insisting she drive us to her parent's dacha. Though a university lecturer she did two jobs to supplement an inadequate salary. I learned this is common practice, and necessary, among government employees in Russia.

In country air, and clear light at the dacha we enjoyed a memorable, jovial, barbecue and something strange occurred when I was with Yuri. Although my Russian is not fluent I understood everything he was telling me and so much it

St Elijah the Prophet Church, Yaroslavl.

Yaroslavl's tree lined Volga Embankment.

Neglected Church Complex, Yaroslavl.

Remarkable Museum of Music and Time, Yaroslavl.

Yaroslval's Kremlin Russian Bear.

Tolgsky Monastery from the Volga River.

Rostov's Kremlin and Cathedral.

Vlasyevskaya Tower, Yaroslavl.

148

it was inexplicable.

 Returning home Sveta stopped at Yaroslavl train station where I purchased a ticket to return to Petersburg the following Friday. She was disappointed I was leaving so soon and wanting to show me more of Yaroslavl. I had begun to realise however that I was a burden to them. She worked hard and badly needed weekends to recuperate. Kate had become unfriendly and decidedly moody.

The following day I explored Yaroslavl on my own and with an inadequate map, I'd purchased from a small stationery shop, I strolled from to the city centre, in search of Yaroslavl's renowned theatre district.

Yaroslavl theatre, one of the oldest in Russia, was founded in the 18th century by an actor, Fyodor Volkov, a stepson of a Kostroma city merchant. Volkov opened his theatre when he was 21 years old. It soon became so successful it was attended by the glamorous, Russian Empress, Elizabeth who in admiration asked him to help in starting her own theatre in Petersburg.

The present theatre, a yellow painted building, was built in 1911, before the Revolution, but nevertheless still designed with the distinctive, palpable Soviet rigidity. Inside, its cold orderliness, confirmed my first impression. Probably the 19th century theatre would have been less austere and filled with Bohemian warmth as it training some of Russia's finest actors. It maintained its reputation and has withstood all the ravage, and ruthless decades, of change and still offers the public international as well as Russian plays.

Whether they were with the theatre I don't know but in the streets close by the theatre I saw some of the prettiest women I have ever seen anywhere. It shouldn't have surprised me. All of the Volga River's historic cities are celebrated for their beautiful women and it was often commented on by 18th century travellers.

Hearing I had explored the city alone Sveta went to Kate's room to speak to her and found her moody daughter had, that day, experienced her first sign of puberty. In emotional turmoil Kate cried to her mother that she didn't have a father of her own. Now I understood that quiet, unspoken weariness, and isolation, she had tried to hide that filled me with protective concern for her.

Sveta, with her limitless, driven energy that always exuded clouds of anxiety, decided to leave Kate alone to herself. We visited a museum, which unfortunately was within thirty minutes of closing. Sveta had wanted me to see some rare archaeological finds, of the Yaroslav area, dating back thousands of years. The region once had a thriving settlement of Meyra, a Finnic tribe, 6000 years ago and surprisingly remnants of this ethnic group still live in Russia today.

Indefatigable, though the evening was late, Sveta then drove 37 miles to Rostov Veliky, one of the earliest towns in Russia, founded by the Meyra's. Some historians thought it was founded by Vikings, in the 9th century, but there are records from that period describing it as an already thriving city.

Rostov's medieval Kremlin, and fortified city centre, is rated second only to Moscow's own great Kremlin. It is a dreamlike city, of ancient churches and historic buildings, built on the banks of Lake Nero, an eight mile long pre-ice age lake, estimated to be half a million years old. Due to its high phosphorus, and nitrogen content, the lake is abundant with fish and an anglers dream. It was late in the evening so we had no chance to view the lake or enjoy a boat ride across it or see inside Rostov's remarkable, gleaming, historic Kremlin. All I could see before me were its towering turban domes pointing, like missiles, towards a purple turning evening sky.

Outside the impressive Kremlin walls, in the falling sun, a street market of hand crafts was still selling gifts. Rostov, a major tourist attraction of Russia's Golden Ring, is a haven for market vendors. Unlike the usual, down-trodden, city marketers I had become used to these were confident, cheerful and unhurried in their efforts to close for the day. Seeing me watching they shuffled in front of me their best items. Browsing I noticed a pretty bracelet and necklace and purchased it as a gift for Klaudia, Sveta's mother and noticing a decorative box purchased it for Kate.

Northern Russia has, since medieval times, a thriving and well known enamel industry which had been the basis of the Stroganoff family's fabulous wealth so for myself I chose a blemish-free, wall ceramic, depicting Rostov's Assumption Cathedral. The Cathedral has some of the largest bells in Russia cast in 16th century and it was a favourite place of the deranged Ivan the Terrible. I regretted not being able to visit it.

Journeying home to Yaroslavl, Sveta, decided to stop and fill her car with petrol. In Russia it is usual to inform the petrol attendant the amount of fuel one wants to purchase, then pay for it before going to the pump, done of course to prevent theft of fuel. I offered to pay and Sveta began to fill the tank but she had over-estimated. Soon her car fuel tank filled to overflow and began to jettison fuel, from the delivery pump nozzle, like a hose pipe. Two Russian men shouted to her 'Over here, over here,' hoping she would put the excess fuel in their car.

The next day I was still quite ill and had lost considerable weight. All desire for food had left me. Kate morosely silent didn't want us to stay at home. At mid-morning we visited an Art Gallery to see an exhibition, of Hogarth engravings, on loan from London. Kate was not impressed, looking askance at

Hogarth's sceptical depictions of marriage, perhaps recalling the divorce of her parents. We came home early so I did my laundry, by hand, because there was no washing machine and to dry my clothes I hung them in the sunshine filling my bedroom window.

Sveta arriving early, from lectures, rushed us off to see the internationally acclaimed Tolgsky Convent. This lovely place had been founded, as a monastery, in the 14th century at the place a Bishop of the Church had seen a miracle, the appearance of an icon of the Virgin Mary and Child in a column of fire and he took the icon with him. After this supernatural event the monastery became famous and the miraculous icon became an instrument of healing. Many Russians claimed to have been healed by it including Ivan the Terrible. Thereafter Russian Imperial families, throughout the centuries, visited Tolgsky Monastery. The last Tsar, Nicholas 11, and his family, visited in 1913 no doubt seeking healing for their haemophiliac son Prince Alexei.

After the Revolution the monastery was closed. All services there were forbidden by the Soviets by 1928. These stately historic buildings were then allowed to fall into ruin until in 1987 a program of reconstruction began and the revered monastery was reopened but this time as a convent. In 2003 the revered miraculous icon 'Our Lady of Tolga,' was returned to the Convent.

Sveta had driven us to the Convent but thought I should return with Kate, by ferry, on the serene Volga, a journey of one hour, to the river port at Yaroslavl. To be on the beloved Volga again I just couldn't resist.

From the ferry I could see the reflected white of the 350 years old historic Holy Gates of the convent and St Nicholas Church beyond them and never forgot the scene.

Ferries run from Yaroslavl Port to Tolgsky five times per day. A ferry was already waiting when we approached the landing stage. Kate seemed brighter and quietly, shyly, apologised, 'Edward, I am very sorry for my behaviour over the past few days.'

'Kate I am sure it isn't your fault. You are so young to spend all day with a foreigner and having to translate for hours when you are not well,' I replied, genuinely.

The ferry journey was leisurely, soothing, enjoyable and truly Russian. Gulls, flying beside us, paced us all the way to the city and all the ferry passengers appeared to be working class devout Russians.

For seven decades Russians had hidden their innate spirituality, throughout the Soviet period, secretly hiding their revered icons and praying alone before them. This spirituality has now sprung to life again, in the freedom of a new Russia that recognises and allows it. Putin, like all Tsars, kisses icons and often consults Church leaders.

Sveta had gone back to the convent to buy an icon and a neck-cross for me, made from wood of the sacred trees of Tolga Convent as a surprise and she was now waiting for us, smiling, at the ferry port. With these gifts she gave me a booklet of the Monastery and Convent history. Hearing I had left my baseball cap at their parent's dacha she and Kate left me at the flat and drove 35 miles to their dacha to get it for me. I doubt if any other people, I had met, anywhere in the world would have gone to this kind of effort and I found it typical Russian hospitality.

That day Marina rang from Petersburg to remind me they were waiting eagerly for my return and were missing my company.

Waking, the following morning, it was obvious my guide Kate, dejectedly miserable, was in no state to accompany me so I set off alone to explore.

Walking along Sovietskaya Street, on the corner of Kedrova Street I saw a yellow building with a large marble statue of a nude female. This surprised me because I hadn't seen many such figures in Russia. Such isolated beauty on a quiet suburban street appeared incongruous. When I later mentioned it to Sveta she told me, 'When I was a girl I would always stop to look at it in admiration and wonder.'

My walk took me to St Blasé Tower, a solid, powerful looking, thick walled, 17th century structure, which had been part of Yaroslavl's town fortifications.

Strolling further on I discovered many historic, deserted churches with their massive doors locked, looking sadly forlorn and forgotten, not only by Russians, but by God himself.

I browsed city shops just to look around but, unlike Petersburg, but could find no one in them that spoke English.

When I returned late afternoon Sveta suggested I should to see her parents, for the last time, at their dacha. The weather sympathised with my mood as we drove beneath dark clouds weeping in a persistent downpour of heavy rain. It was a sad moment for me aware I might never see them again. I had begun to experience that sense of belonging as though they were my own family.

Klaudia, Sveta's mother, was genuinely delighted at my gifts of ring, necklace, bracelet and ear-rings. I gave Sveta $100 to purchase a mobile phone for her father Yuri. He needed one urgently because of his faltering health and prolonged heart condition. For Kate I gave a gift to celebrate her advent into womanhood. We all hugged, Russian style, and that was the last I ever saw of Sveta's parents.

Sveta with Kate drove me to the railway station the following evening. We were early for my 10.20 pm train so we dashed over to see Sveta's sister, whom I had never met, working at an open air bar on the banks of the Kotorosl River.

Back at the rail station Sveta helped me find my sleeper carriage. We were both surprised to find that on this occasion my companion, in the opposite bunk, was an elegant, fashionably dressed, pretty woman in her forties.

Calling the conductress the female companion remonstrated at having to share the carriage with a man. The conductress spoke to her politely. I didn't understand what was said but the woman soon became calm when she understood I was English. She seemed to generously accept she would be quite safe in my company.

During the night my companion, on the other side of the carriage, disturbed me by getting up, to remove her cotton top and pyjama trousers. Our carriage was too warm she thought. After this unreserved disrobing she fell back onto her bed and fell asleep. Later when I turned in my bunk I saw she had only partly covered herself with a blanket, leaving one leg fully exposed, and revealing brilliantly white, pretty lace panties. Turning away I too fell asleep.

At 7.00 am sharp we were woken by a train attendant bringing coffee. Opening the carriage window curtains I saw a morning cloudlessly sunny. Villages, forests and lakes sped past in, lonely isolation, until we entered Petersburg's city outskirts at 11.00 am.

INHERIT THE WIND

Wishing my companion farewell I alighted in Petersburg and eventually saw Marina, who walked passed me, not recognising me, I had lost so much weight in Yaroslavl.

At Victoria's flat Marina had a bottle of Moscow champagne to celebrate my safe return. Lara had been ill all the time I had been away.

The next was sunny so, we set off to find the real place where, I was sure, the assassinated Rasputin had been thrown off a bridge to hide his murder.

Books I had read about this incident claimed he had been thrown into the Moika Canal. This didn't agree at all with him being tossed into the Baltic in the belief his body would flow out to sea. Personally I was sure it had been from a bridge on Krestovsky Island, an area of parks and woodland, from which there were fine views of the Gulf of Finland.

The island is now an untidy place of boatyards. I thought it a dangerous place to be. Part of the island has been converted into a shabby, untidy and chaotic amusement park.

Rasputin has been much maligned by writers and I believe quite incorrectly. Those who knew him well described him as a gentle person with a great love of nature. It was said he didn't like to even tread on wild flowers. He was a travelling preacher described as having, "a sense of calm, gentle strength and warmth of conviction". It was without doubt one reason the Imperial family took to him so easily.

Deeply religious, from childhood, Rasputin had become a monk but deserted the monastery, he had joined, in disgust at their homosexuality. From there he walked from the far reaches of Siberia to Petersburg not at all an easy journey. In petersburg Russian Orthodox Bishops recognised his spirituality, gifts of healing and prophesy seeing them as gifts of the Holy Spirit, mentioned in the New Testament and it was the Orthodox Church that recommended him to Nicholas the Second.

Empress Alexandra, a devout Christian, believed in Rasputin's powers and they soon became friends. Such friendship, and closeness with the Imperial family, aroused dangerous envy and rivalry, among Church leaders and nobility, during this time of simmering rebellion and desire for political change in Russia. On one occasion, in jealous rage, a Bishop of the Church beat Rasputin with a wooden cross. The disgruntled population, of Petersburg and Moscow, were seeking a scapegoat. Newspapers began printing stories of Rasputin's debauchery and affairs with women of the nobility, none of which was true. Rasputin in fact didn't drink alcohol, until in his forties and then only for pain relief after a female assassin, posing as a beggar to whom he stopped to give money, stabbed him in the stomach so severely that he required surgery. He was never, physically, quite the same afterwards.

Secret police were sent to spy on Rasputin, to discredit him. Finding no evidence they wrote fictitious reports to Tsar Nicholas. In one they claimed, when he was drunken in a bar, he exposed himself to a group of women. When Tsar Nicholas read it he pointed out, to the Chief of Police, that it couldn't be true since at that time Rasputin was in the Royal Palace of Tsarskoe Selo. Fake news isn't a modern phenomenon.

Failure in war, and not giving Russian people the democracy they sought meant Nicholas was in disfavour. People wishing for change blamed Rasputin who in their eyes had become, with the German born Empress, the reason for all of Russia's problems. It was even rumoured Rasputin was sleeping with Empress Alexandra and her daughters, which any thoughtful person would have known could not be true.

Rasputin, as church and Imperial Family believed, did have a gift of healing. When doctors failed to help Nicholas' son Alexei, a haemophiliac, Rasputin was able to stop his fatal bleeding episodes with just a few words. The monk also had prophetic gifts he had warned the Tsar not to go to war with Germany because it would fail and he was correct. In a premonition of his own murder, by a member of the nobility, he told Tsar Nicholas that if any member of the nobility assassinated him it would result in the end of the monarchy, and time gave truth to his words.

Mixed into this explosive, powder keg scenario, was the strange, bi-sexual, dissolute, Prince Felix Yusupov, a man whom in his youth had enjoyed cross dressing.

The Yusupovs were one of the richest families in Russia, with greater wealth than even the Tsar. They owned 675,000 acres of land on which were kept more than 40,000 serfs, and supported dozens of businesses. At the time of Rasputin's murder Felix Yusupov lived in his grand palace on the Moika Canal in Petersburg.

Prince Felix' brother Nicolai, at 26 years, was unwise to have an affair with a married woman, a common practice in Petersburg society. On this occasion her husband killed him, in a duel, on the very island where Felix and his murderous companions, I believe, tossed the body of Rasputin into the winter ice below Krestovsky Bridge.

Obtaining a portrait of Felix Yusupov I placed a small mirror down its centre to replicate the two facial halves of his personality and was truly surprised by what I saw. There were two entirely different images, one revealing an evil, cruel visage, the other a gentle and mild personality. It was like gazing at two different people, Cain and Abel inside one man.

Felix had married a niece of Nichols II, Irina Alexandrovna Romanova, a granddaughter of Nicholas I. He had been immediately attracted to her when they first met, no doubt because of her cold, androgynous appearance. She could easily have passed as a young male and Irina became even more masculine looking, her portraits reveal, as she grew older. Like everyone in her circle she knew of Felix' homosexuality but didn't find it unattractive. Her own father had been a serial adulterer in Petersburg's privileged society where there were no sexual mores or prohibitions.

It is hard to imagine what persuaded Felix to murder Rasputin, he must have known Tsar Nicholas and Alexandra would be incensed by it, but Yusupov was of a wealthy, spoiled nobility who thought they could do anything, and get away with it, just as French nobility had prior to their own bloody revolution.

Yusupov invited Rasputin, on 30th December 1916, to his Moika Palace on the pretext of meeting his pretty wife Irina. On arrival Rasputin was shown into a small basement room, as though he were an unwelcome tradesman. No setting could have been more incongruous, the poor peasant, holy man and one of Russia's most powerful and richest nobles. In a way it was an image of Russia at the time.

What happened next is well known. Rasputin, it is said, had a premonition he was to be murdered that night. His daughter Matrena, the only survivor of his four children to escape the Revolution horrors, wrote that she survived because Rasputin had told her, "Run and run fast, while you still can"

Fleeing, as her father had advised, Matrena, after years of travel through Russia and Europe, settled in Paris.

After poisoning, shooting, and beating him the assassins threw Rasputin's corpse into the river expecting his body to float away into the Baltic but instead Rasputin's body floated back towards Petersburg on the Malaya Neva.

Hearing of it the Empress heartbroken remarked she had, 'lost her only comfort and friend.'

As a member of nobility, married to the Tsars niece, Yusupov was able to escape punishment for this murder. He was banished to the Crimea, which he didn't like, and in less than one year quietly returned to revolutionary Petersburg where realising the extent of the revolutionary danger all around, fled and settled in Paris where he lived, flamboyantly, until his death at the age of 80 years.

The dissembling Russian press however still wouldn't leave poor Rasputin in peace. They published fake stories saying one of the royal princesses, Tatiana, went to Rasputin's body and cut off his penis, in anger at his attempted sexual violation of her and his penis, fictitiously, is said to be preserved in a glass jar in Petersburg.

There is a new bridge on Krestovsky Island but I managed to find the original 1843 wooden one from which I believe Rasputin had been thrown into the winter ice. The location was troubling and decayed, the day heavy, beneath a grey sky, a dismal place in keeping with such an ignoble act.

We returned to the island amusement park where Lara, in spite of illness, energetically played at everything within reach.

One day I decided to visit St. Isaacs Cathedral on Admiralty Prospekt. It was not difficult to find, its massive golden dome, clearly visible in Petersburg, shines brightly from 220 lbs of gold leaf overlaying it.

St. Isaacs, the third largest Cathedral in the world, is named after Saint Isaac of Dalmatia, who was born the same birth date as Peter the Great. It is customary in Russia, to this day, to adopt a saint as your favourite if you share a common birthdate. St Isaacs took more than forty years to construct and is a pleasing sight. Its construction exacted a large death toll, like a biblical sacrifice. Some sixty men died from mercury vapour poisoning alone while gilding its massive dome in addition to many other fatalities.

Inside the Cathedral are approximately 60 murals and 150 oil paintings. The iconostasis, is faced with white marble, ten green malachite pillars and two of blue lazurite and it is magnificent. Yet for all that there is no sense of holiness in this place, it is just a show case of Russian architecture, aesthetics, and a monument to Peter the Great. In keeping with this view, in 1931 it became a museum. In 1941-45 it was badly damaged by German bombardment. The moment war ended its restoration began and it is now once more shining in its soulless, glory.

The Cathedral's, gilt bronze, Holy Doors, in the iconostasis, weigh five tons and the iconostasis first and second tiers of icons are wonderful mosaics, so perfectly executed, it is difficult to realise they are mosaic. Above them, on a third tier, are oil paintings depicting saints and patriarchs of the Old Testament. Beyond the Holy Doors is a stained glass window, quite unusual in Russia since stained glass is not a preference in their churches or cathedrals, depicting a risen Christ that strangely, resembles the young Rasputin. There are two side chapels, St. Catherine's and St. Alexander Nevsky's, with wonderful white marble faced iconostasis.

After St. Isaacs I wanted to see the sumptuous palace of the perpetrator of

Rasputin's murder. We walked to Moika Canal to find house number 94.

Yusupov Palace is a grand, yellow painted building, facing the Moika embankment, easily distinguished by six columns at its entrance. Its outside appearance conveys no suggestion of the luxuriance found inside. The building was owned and first lived in by Prince Nickolai Yusupov, an accomplished diplomat and art collector. This talented Prince who spoke five languages fluently was a favourite courtier of Catherine the Great, Tsar Paul and Tsar Alexander I. Nickolai an inveterate traveller befriended many of the most famous people in Europe. Recognising his love of art the Imperial family appointed him to choose valuable items for the Hermitage, Tsarskoe Selo and their Royal Palace at Gatchina, eventually making him director of the Hermitage.

The Yusupov's, descended from Tartar Muslims began accumulating their enormous fortune under Ivan the Terrible when they converted to Christianity but it was wealth reputed to be based on persistent theft and murder. If that sounds familiarly like New Russian oligarchy you are correct. Their Palace had been built in 1760 and Nickolai, turned its interior into one of the most elegant in all of Petersburg. His son Boris later continued this expansion after his father's death.

Felix Yusupov, Rasputin's murderer, had inherited this dazzling edifice after his older brother was killed in a duel. Felix married Irina Romanov, granddaughter of Tsar Alexander III and niece of Nicholas II. They had met after he had studied at Oxford University 1909-1913, where he was remembered for his lavish lifestyle, drug addiction, and membership of the Bullingdon Club, the favourite of Tory elite politicians.

Entering Yusupov Palace visitors are confronted by a graceful staircase, lit by an enormous crystal chandelier. Climbing these historic stairs leads to a sparse lobby waiting room with straight back chairs thrust against its walls. Past this uninteresting room you enter more elegant, compact rooms; Green Drawing Room with desk, a harp and large chandelier; Red Drawing Room filled with red chairs and red silk panel walls. Then Blue Drawing Room, which I thought the most beautiful of all, with blue chairs, white marble and blue fabric walls, lit by gilded angel, candle light stands. Beyond these sumptuous rooms is a large rotunda, encircled with eight marble columns supporting a cupola representing the heavens. Leaving this we come to a small, intimate, ballroom with grand piano and above it all another huge chandelier, with 132 lights, reflecting light to walls and dazzling mirrors, that give width and depth to the room.

Gazing round, absorbing its opulence, I sensed an air of sadness hanging like a diaphanous cloud over it all. Further a spacious banqueting room was supported by twelve marble columns and at the head of it a sculpture of the Greek god Dionysus, god of wine, fertility, drama and debauchery. A series of halls leads to a delightful small theatre, with two tiers of balconies each side of the stalls. It had been built in 1840 to imitate the theatres of Europe. Performances are still held here.

Princess Irina Yusupov's apartments, and bedroom, are in blue décor with matching blue chairs. Prince Felix's own apartments include study and library and a smoking room for his close, licentious, friends. In these Felix had an oriental room, with marble swimming pool, where he sometimes, discarding concerns of privilege, relaxed dressed in his mother's jewels, imagining he was surrounded by naked, black Moorish slaves. It all gives a glimpse into the mind of this indolent prince, who was so powerful he was beyond law or morality.

The most popular room, in the palace, is not found in these upper, extra elegant, grand spaces but in the basement where Felix, in keeping with his aberrant predilections, kept a small private apartment for his decadent friends. It is the place to which he lured Rasputin, to sit at table and await a supposed meeting with Princess Irina. Three of Felix's friends, Grand Duke Dimitri Romanov, Dr Stanislaus Lazovert and Vladimir Pushkevich were there to help Felix murder Rasputin.

In this sparse basement is an exhibition, of that treacherous murder, showing effigies of Rasputin and the arrogant, malevolent, conspirators with a date given as 17th December 1916 not 30th as is often claimed.

I left Yusupov Palace feeling depressed realising that for all its grandeur, despair seeped from its walls. If anyone believes in universal justice this place reveals a different story, none of the perpetrators were brought to account and all escaped the horrors of the Revolution. .

Another day I visited the Ethnographic Museum I had read so much about, and set off on a fine morning that quickly turned to absolutely torrential rain. On arrival I found the museum closed that day.

Travelling by Petersburg's trams that I enjoyed so much, I noticed that when we passed a Church, Marina would make a sign of the cross, so I asked her about this because she didn't seem to be religious in any way.

Without looking at me, Marina replied, 'Russians often do this, not out of respect for our Church but to ask God for protection against the Church. Throughout history we have been subjugated and oppressed by the Church. It was why Stalin was so against religion, as a tool of the Tsars.'

In stores on Nevsky Prospect I was frequently bullied by other shoppers. Russians just push you out of the way if they wish to look at some item. They do it, without animosity, as part of Russian behaviour. Marina found my disgust and surprise amusing whenever it happened to me.

'It's normal,' she shrugged.

Behaviour of this kind gives a glimpse into Russian psyche. They lack empathy, a legacy of Communism. It's displayed in every walk of life and a reason for a willingness to accept, and partake, in every form of corruption.

I had seen so much of touristy parts of Petersburg and was aware they showed me nothing of what life was really like for Russians living in this unique and beautiful city. Mentioning this to Marina she and Lara began to show me places, outside of these tourist venues, favoured, and frequented, by ordinary Pitertsy (People of Petersburg).

A place to begin would be the flat, she and Lara occupied, in the Proletariat (Workers) area of the city.

I had seen in Samara how some pensioners lived in single, constricted, ten by eight rooms, worse than prison cells. Now I would see how Soviet so called equality had housed its working class.

Russian socialism never meant a classless society. There was always an enormous gap between Soviet elite and the majority of people. In Communism privileged nobility was just replaced by advantaged politicians, party members, and factory managers. As they always had the majority of Russians lived in the poorest of cramped conditions.

The Proletariat area of Petersburg fascinated me. It has an appealing beauty, in its dilapidation, which somehow gives the district magnetic grandeur. If you like the paintings of J.S. Lowry you would love this part of Petersburg.

We walked, from a tram stop, across a waste ground of mud puddles and

wild grass to a complex of five storey flats. Spaces between these blocks had
become a chaotic muddle of dilapidated cars. Grass verges were protected with
worn out car tyres dividing road, from unkempt lawns, preventing parking.
Dogs wandered round dejectedly, litter cringed and blew over the grass.

The flats, were neglected in appearance. Weather stains disfigured the
rendering of shabby walls. Marina's flat on a fourth floor was reached by
stairs and a cramped dirty lift that was slow and smelled of urine mingled with
nicotine. There were four flats to each floor; corridors were dismal in
appearance and without much light and inside Marina's flat I was further
dismayed by what I saw.

Marina and Lara lived in one room. Lara had never, in all her life, had her
own bedroom. In place of one, her mother had strung a line across the room,
from which hung a curtain, behind which, Lara had an inadequate semblance
of privacy, and a tiny bunk to sleep on. Marina's own bed was sagging and
must have been painful to sleep on. In a small cubicle off their living room
was a shower, without a curtain. A washbasin, drooping from adjoining wall,
was held in place by a wobbly plumbing pipe beneath it. On the bathroom wall
I noticed a large cockroach.

To make its cramped dilapidation a happier place Marina had painted, on
the doors, quite skilfully, accurately and beautifully, characters from Walt
Disney films. Lara, for company, had a pet tortoise that followed her
everywhere like a dog.

These worker flats were constructed in 1953 on the orders of Nikita
Khrushchev, the Soviet leader, and became known as Khruschyoka, communal
living. They were built, with poor quality low cost concrete, for workers and
non-party residents. Their name soon changed to 'Khruschoba' meaning

Khrushchev's slums.

British Labour Prime Minister, Harold Wilson, thought them such a good cheap concept he introduced them, with slightly different design, in Britain and, like their Russian predecessors, they too soon fell into disrepute. In America President Donald Trump's father became exceedingly wealthy by using the sameconcept.

Everywhere these shoddy blocks have been built they have demeaned the lives of occupants and resulted in high crime rates, drug addiction and despair. No one ever considered their effect on the unfortunate peoples forced to live in them.

The Proletariat areas of Petersburg, filled with these monstrosities, have reached the end of their useful life. They had been intended to last for 25 years but still remain fifty years later. President Putin is determined to replace them and has begun slowly demolishing them.

Outside, between the run down blocks of flats, Marina walked with me to a small grocery store where I purchased groceries. Whatever I bought, other shoppers came to see. When I asked Marina about this she replied, 'They know you are a foreigner and think if you buy something it must be of the finest quality and the best thing to buy.'

It wasn't all miserable dilapidation in Prolatetsia. Nature strives to heal scars and brings life into even the most deadly wounds. Between the wretched grey utility and monotony wild lawns were filled with balsamic poplars scenting the air and filling the sky with cotton wool balls that fell, sleepily to cover grass, and clothes, like snow fall. It was Stalin himself who encouraged planting these poplars because they were incendiary and believed they could be used in armaments. Poplar cotton balls are so flammable Russian children gather them, in mischievous piles, to set fire to them.

By nature reticent, and anxious, Marina this day, more trusting and talkative, began to tell me about herself.

'I have been married twice but my first husband, Lara's father, died when he was only thirty.' Marina stared, sadly downwards. 'He suffered badly from depression and became alcoholic. Sometimes he wept in his terrible misery. Eventually, when Lara was still a baby, unable to cope with it, I left him and then he died tragically. Police found him hanging in his flat. There wasn't a note to anyone. His photos and identity passport had been thrown into a fire stove. Police believed he was murdered by Chechens.' Marina paused, her face cold with anger. 'They are all criminals, they make and sell toxic alcohol. It is believed that's what killed him. Then the Chechens tried to cover it up by hanging him and burning all his identity. I feel tormented by it, so much. If I hadn't left him perhaps it would never have happened.'

Marina was on the verge of tears. We walked silently, after this, over the tired pavements and the slumping grass of the Proleteriat.

On one occasion I noticed Marina, sometime in life, had badly broken her arm, that hadn't set perfectly, so I asked her about it.

'Well one day, when I was young I fell, and broke it, but didn't tell anyone. At home my mother saw me holding my arm, the bone was sticking out of the skin. She rushed me to a hospital but it wasn't repaired very well. I often fell over, as a child, and once so heavily I broke my tail bone. It was so badly damaged they had to operate to repair it.'

Marina spoke without emotion but underneath it all I saw she was constantly anxious and her fingers never still.

'After school what did you do as a career?' I asked.

'During the Soviet period all school children were streamlined into careers. They advised me to enter the construction industry. There was complete male and female equality in Russia. I studied and gained a diploma in architecture. Many women in Russia worked in construction. It was a hands on job. A doctor once told me that someone with such delicate hands as mine should never be doing that kind of work and it is true I am much more skilled in art and creating things, but no one cared.'

'Are you in a happy marriage now?' I asked pryingly.

Marina looked at me and smiled. 'He is a good man but, as a colonel, he is often away in Moscow where sometimes we live. I met him, and fell in love, but no one is ever happy in Russia no matter what life brings.'

I asked about living in this workers area, the proletariat district.

'The place is filled with addicts and thieves and mafia Chechens. Everything is falling to bits. It's expected all these flats will be knocked down. Balconies are crumbling. They sometimes just fall into the street. Luckily it happens mostly at night but I'm always careful walking on the path near our flats.'

During times I explored the area, I noticed it was often devoid people and roamed by unkempt dogs. Marina strolled with me past warehouse buildings, and former offices, without windows, all left emptily derelict. The area must once have been thriving but not now, the fall of Communism changed all that.

Evening came, Lara joined us from school, so the three of us walked a deserted park nearby. It was beautiful, as all Russian parks are, and well maintained, even here among empty warehouses and dismal, decaying Khrushchev flats. In the empty loneliness we could hear trills of bird song bringing sound and life to the forgotten world of Proletariatskaya. I searched for them but couldn't see any of these shy, melodious birds.

'Marina, what are those birds?' I asked.

Opening her shoulder bag, to look through her Russian-English dictionary, Marina replied, 'Nightingales.'

They were Thrush Nightingales, found throughout Russia, and one of the most enchanting of song birds. There is beauty and hope, even in the most dire of circumstances, if you are willing to notice. Everything about that sad day changed for me with birdsong and Lara's playful energy.

From a broad, untidy street near this empty park, we caught a tram to visit an unusual, and delightful ethnic restaurant named, 'Karavan Sarai'. This popular Uzbek diner, on Nekrasova Sreet, served oriental cuisine. Through its doors everything sparkled with exotic décor.

'It's a place', Marina said, 'Known for its marvellous soups.'

Returning late, to Marina's flat, Maina confided, 'I hate this place. One day, coming home, I noticed an awful stench coming from under the door of the flat next to mine. An old lady lived there. She had a son, but he never came to visit much, so I rang the police. When they got inside they found her dead. She had been dead for two weeks.' Marina, despondently raising eyes in despair, added, 'This happens in Russia. If you are poor, you aren't just a number, you are a nobody.'

'Let's go back to my flat,' I encouraged, so after picking up a few things, we left.

The flat I had rented was ample for all of us. Its owner, Victoria, a Soviet sporting champion, had been given, in appreciation of her achievement, this large, 150 square metres, residence in a wealthy area. It turned out to be one of the strangest places I have ever lived in.

Until staying in this apartment I had never believed in ghosts, or that buildings could be haunted. This place changed my mind. We had already experienced problems with its water supply that no one else in this building had encountered. I often found the apartment unexplainably cold.

One night the light shade, in the living room, was rocking from side to side. I conjectured it must be caused by vibrations from the flat above us but later, when I went to my bedroom, it happened with that ceiling light also and so, violently I though it an Earth tremor. There didn't seem to be logical explanation for it. I was sure the flat owner knew about these strange occurrences because, when Marina rang her to mention it, the owner replied that a man in the flat above ours often came home drunk and began pulling the electricity wires. This I found hard to believe since these flats, sturdily built, had superb sound proofing and concrete floors. How anyone could have got to the wiring in a flat below was beyond reason.

I purchased a heater to ameliorate the cold in the flat but it made no difference, it was always close to freezing. We had to learn to live with it.

A growing delight, for me, was visiting Petrograd Island, across the Neva. Its main thoroughfare, Kamennoostravsky Prospect, is flanked by splendid art nouveau buildings. Petrograd is a preferred quarter for wealthy 'New Russians' who like to live beside Petrograd's musicians, actors and writers. It is a Bohemian place of classy, charming cafes, restaurants and galleries and I would have loved to live there myself.

The obsessively compulsive, troubled and celebrated Soviet composer Shostakovich, who smoked and drank himself to death, lived here. Russia's famous poet, Pushkin, had studied on Petrograd at the Lyceum. One of Russia's most beautiful and talented ballerinas, Matilda Kshesinskaya, lived in the once prominent Petrograd building, named after her, the Kshesinskaya Mansion. Matilda apart from ballet fame was also well known for her affair with the last Tsar, Nicholas II, before his marriage to Alexandra. Prudently, when she noticed a dark storm of Revolution approaching she fled, as many wealthy Russians did, to Paris and went on to live to be 99 years old. After the events of 1917, Bolshevik leaders, who for all their rhetoric, loved to live in the grandest of palaces and mansions, used Kshesinkaya's Mansion as a Soviet Elite boozy headquarters.

In Lev Tolstoy Street, close by Kshesinskaya Mansion are expensive shops, theatres and bars that we enjoyed.

One sunny day we visited Petrograd's Botanic Gardens, situated on a small islet known as Apothecary Island. We crossed a bridge over the granite walled, winding river of Karpovka, which is no wider than a canal and only three kilometres long, to reach the famed Garden.

Peter the Great, impressed with exuberant, the exotic gardens of France and Versailles Palace, decided Petersburg also needed an enchanting ornamental garden, and one even better than that of Louis XIV of France. With the extraordinary vigour he showed in everything he attempted Peter planned the gardens himself, hired the finest gardeners, purchased seeds and plants from major botanic centres, and began his project.

By 1710 there were trees, he planted himself, flowers and shrubs, acquired from all over Europe and the East and especially scented ones. To this he added statues sculptured in Italy. A famous French landscaper, Alexandre LeBlond, who had designed Versailles, was invited to Petersburg to assist. This French garden genius sent for even more trees and flowers, built a conservatory, created a garden of fountains, water pyramids and grottos within the garden's thirty seven acres.

From the beginning Peter decided it would be open to the public. Eventually the Botanic garden grew, into what we see today, with an additional 25 greenhouses.

In 1931 the Komarov Botanical Institute was founded as part of this garden complex. There are now approximately 700 plants and 3,500 more in its greenhouses, a garden herbarium, with more than 5 million plants, collected from all over the world, and a plant museum that is one of the largest in Europe.

This was one of the most interesting of my days in Petersburg.

In a greenhouse open to the public, not all of them are unless on guided tours, there were gigantic water lilies and an enormous 160 year old cacti. Peter's Gardens were created to convey the tranquillity, escape and beauty that is own life lacked. That is what you experience here and won't forget, in this secluded haven. Russians have always loved the grandeur of nature around them. Every park and garden, in this enormous country reflects this passion and pride and is shown in maintenance of them to the highest standard.

Back in Petrograd we walked beside another garden. A man, with a horse, was offering to let people ride beside the gardens so I urged Lara to take a ride. At first afraid, when looking at the height of the 16 hand creature, she eventually mounted and paced the garden paths.

Marina with her remarkable observation noticed a famous Russian actor striding into the gardens. She approached him, asking if he was really the famous film star she had seen in so many films. The man stopped, and in the most gentlemanly and noble way, taking off his broad brimmed hat in respect, replied, 'Yes', then spoke with her in kindly, attentive manner for several minutes. He had probably thought that in his baggy trench coat, and slouch hat, no one would recognise him but was then delighted someone did.

Petersburg's local trains and trams became my favourite means of travelling and we returned by them. They don't offer the most comfortable of rides, with their hard seats, and trundling along at 30 miles per hour through city suburbs but they give a chance to see Russians, away from tourist crowds and I found an hypnotic charm in their slow, determined roll and sociability.

One of the delights of Petersburg is Pavlovsk Park, 17 miles south of the city. To visit this unforgettable estate you catch a leisurely local train, filled with Russians, happily chatting, pleased to be free from Petersburg life. One day we did this on the slow train that conveniently stopped opposite the Pavlovsk Park entrance.

Pavlovsk Palace estate is 1500 acres of parkland, unique and celebrated for its beauty and countryside design. Most of Petersburg estates were planned with orderly avenues and grid patterns but Pavlosk was designed to be a natural, landscaped, park garden in English style. Begun when Catherine the Great, celebrating the birth of her first grandson Alexander, gave this former hunting ground, of the Tsars, to her son Paul. She also decided, to celebrate this grandest of occasions, by building a palace on the site for him, his young wife Maria, and their son.

Catherine, in 1782, asked her favourite Scottish architect, Charles Cameron, to design a large palace for Paul. Of course he agreed and filled the estate with statues and the palace with French furniture. Princess Maria however thought Cameron a bit old fashioned, which no doubt he was. She dismissed him and gave the task of building the Palace to Russian born craftsmen. Beautiful as the palace is, with wonderful interiors and aviary, most enjoyment comes from the matchless park itself.

From the railway station Pavlovsk Park entrance is a wide avenue of enormous trees, planned to impress nobility, and the affluent, that visited in their liveried carriages, or horseback and troika sledge from all Europe. There is a sense of playful tranquility in the park, with its surprises of undulating meadows, waterways and rustic bridges. There are rowing boats to hire which we did before walking through the park'-s towering trees.

At a bike stop, near the approach to the estate, we hired bicycles to ride through long avenues, beside pavilions, an Apollo Colonnade and splendid bridges. One pavilion, had been a favourite of Princess Maria who had held literary evenings and concerts there. Further on is a circle of statues depicting the nine muses. Even by bike we never saw all of this gigantic park, which is approximately two and a half square miles, because there was so much to see along its winding paths. I have never enjoyed so much, in all my travels, any park the way I did this one.

Vasilevskiy Island, another part of Petersburg I had read much about, was on my agenda to see. It had been Peter the Great's intention that Vasilevskiy Island would become the Administrative Centre of Petersburg. It didn't happen, for all his frustrated planning, due to it being the lowest level part of his planned metropolis. The island, in Peter's day, was prone to exasperating annual floods, inundating the Island caused by the turbulent waters of the Small and Great Neva Rivers that meet there. Instead of becoming Petersburg's Administrative Centre it became a port that drew in many German mercantile settlers. Their historic presence is still seen on Vasilevskiy in its Lutheran Churches. Entering one of these you immediately notice the contrast between their Germanic austerity and the flowing design, colour and art of

Slavic Orthodox churches. It is an observable reminder of the chasm lying between Western minds and the creative exuberance of the Slav.

All cities, and communities, develop a soul of their own. Vasilievsky reveals its nature in a confusion of tangled buildings that somehow never manage to synchronise. The island has Twelve Colleges, which now house Petersburg University and the Kunstkammer, a museum, in which some of Peter the Great's most bizarre specimens are kept. Next to it is a Zoological Museum, with the largest collection of specimens in the world, preserving one and a half million items, including a stuffed horse that in better days had been the mount of Peter the Great, at the Battle of Poltava.

There is also a Naval Museum, housed in the former Petersburg Stock Exchange, overlooking the Neva and in view of the Winter Palace. This building, in Greek revival style has two remarkable columns, coloured red, that had once been built as lighthouses in 1811 to guide ships to port along the broad Neva. At 105 feet high they look nothing like any lighthouse I ever saw more like something from a sci-fi phantasy. Occasionally these columns are lit by gas torches to send light, shimmering eerily, over the great river. At the base of these columns are four statues representing the great rivers of Russia, Volga, Dnieper, Neva and Volkhov.

Inside the Naval Museum, built to fanfare the Glory of Russia's Navy, are 1,500 models, some of them enormous, of ships and weaponry used throughout Russia's turbulent history. One can also find documents here recording all of Russia's naval warfare.

The most unexpected sight, near the Naval Museum are two pink, 2,500 years old sphinxes, outside the Academy of Arts. They were found in Nile mud at Thebes in 1820 and Russia purchased them in 1831.

Yusupov Palace, Petersburg

Yusupov Palace display of Rasputin on the night of his murder.

Russia's most celebrated, brilliant and tragic poet, Pushkin.

Peter the Great's Sailing Dinghy.

Cossack heritage still lingers on in Petersburg.

Two Russian Bears near Winter Palace, Petersburg.

Vasilievsky Island is the intellectual centre of Petersburg. It's 'Twelve Colleges' with huge frontage 1,300 feet long have educated some of the greatest of Russia's achievers, the most well-known being Dimitry Mendelev who discovered the periodicity of chemical elements. Lenin also studied here and gained a first.

'Does your husband like working in the military?' I asked Marina during our visit to the museum.

'Not really, but it's his job. He is a colonel after all, and that's a real achievement but his only topic of conversation is his work.'

Marina looked at her troubled hands. Raising her head looking directly at me, she asked, 'Have you heard of dedovshchina?'

'No I don't think so.'

'Do you know we still have military conscription?'

'No, I haven't heard of that.'

'Young men between eighteen and twenty seven have to be in our military for one year. My husband's rank, though quite high, still lets him see the results of the practice of dedovshchina. New recruits are, as a part of initiation, beaten and sometimes seriously. That's what dedovshchina is.'

Marina, continuing to curl her fingers nervously, looked into the distance. 'Sometimes I hate my country and want to leave.'

Dedovshchina was something I had never heard about but when I learned more it shook any rose- tinted views of life in Russia I'd held.

Dedovshchina is inflicted on new recruits by seniors, NCO's and even by officers, as a part of Russia's military training. In essence it is physical, and psychological, abuse and prolonged humiliation. In worse cases recruits have been tortured. The resulting sense of shame, and worthlessness, among these young recruits results in approximately 300-400 suicides per annum. In 2006, 292 young recruits were killed by beatings and torture. When culprits, of these murders, are arrested the crime is military handled and sentences imposed paltry. In exceptional cases a sentence of one year detention is imposed.

In 2012 a conscript, 20 years old, named Ruslan Aiderkhanov was raped and tortured to death by his seniors. The army did their best to cover up the incident. When the young man's coffin was sent home, his parents opened it to find their son's teeth had been knocked out, one eye was missing, his fingers had been hammered, a leg was broken, he had been raped and there were stab wounds to his chest. After enquiries they discovered he had been hung up, with military belts, to make the murder appear to be suicide which his parents had been told was the cause of his death.

The torturers, of this unfortunate youth, were put on trial. The only witness, brave enough to come forward, was later shot dead and the murderers of Ruslan received just one year detention.

A year before this murder another young recruit, named Andrei Sychyov, had been beaten for three hours resulting in broken bones and genital trauma. At the end of his ordeal an army officer ordered him to squat on his haunches, for four hours. Eventually, when he collapsed and was hospitalised both legs had to be amputated, his crushed genitals removed, and his broken bones reset.

To escape this murderous violence, that few other nations would tolerate, many young men avoid conscription by fleeing the country. Is it any wonder, after such brutality and humiliation, that so many Russian men feel worthless and many turn to alcohol, and crime, after they leave military service.

'What does your husband think of this?' I asked.

'He talks about it all the time,' Marina replied obscurely. 'One woman, I know fled with her son to Cyprus. Some families start businesses, open their offices in Europe and take their sons with them. Once there they just keep renewing their visas.'

Changing this depressing subject, Marina suggested I should visit Petersburg's popular markets, in the suburbs.

All over this incredible city there are a variety of street markets that, you come across unexpectedly. Some sell books in English that are classic treasures and I thought quite valuable. Once close to the Hermitage I saw a man selling an album of collectible Russian postage stamps so cheaply I bought it. Food sold at street vendor markets however is questionable and dangerous. One day I purchased meat at one to cook in the evening. It turned out to be so tough that no matter what I did, to make it palatable, nothing worked nor could I chew through it.

Marina laughed, 'In street markets you never know what animal the meat comes from. It could be dog.'

Throughout Russia businesses are forced to pay criminal gangs protection money. I had already observed this in Samara, where I had noticed gang members stationed to watch cafes and street markets. At closure hour they would move in for their cut in profits. Russia's police accept this as part of life and, in some cases, claim their own share from gang masters.

These protection gangs, known as 'the Vor', use enforcers recruited from sportsmen, wrestlers, weight trainers, police and military personnel. By means of local corruption they are able to use blue lights, of police vehicles, on their getaway cars and frequently police moonlight as gang members. At the top of their hierarchy, gang leaders have multi citizenships, of Greece, Ukraine and Israel. This mafia corruption has seen the highest commands of Russia's police, being convicted of fraud, and criminal activities, amounting to hundreds of millions in US dollars.

We saw a brazen example of protection racketeering in Petersburg. On our way home, travelling by tram, we often broke our journey, for coffee, at a small café before catching a Metro home. We did this so frequently the cafe owner presented me with a lapel badge that Marina told me was, 'The communist equivalent of Boy Scouts.' It was a badge of 'Lenin's Young Pioneers.' The business owner did this with all his regular customers. I couldn't decide whether he did it in humour or sarcasm. It was a Soviet era symbol of Lenin's youth movement his 'All Union Pioneer Organisation', in which young members promised to, 'Passionately love the Motherland, to live, study and fight, as the Great Lenin instructed.'

It was a positive brainwashing mantra.

By most standards, the café shabby but the owner likeable and we enjoyed going there. One mid-afternoon I noticed he seemed afraid, when a group of four burly men walked in boozily, arrogantly swaggering, as though the café belonged to them. One of them pushed his hand to the crotch of a young waitress. Neither the owner nor the girl could do anything about it. These offensive bullies ordered coffee and food but made no attempt to pay.

 Marina always seemed to know everything that happened in Petersburg so I asked her quietly, 'Who are these people?'

'They have come for money. We should leave here now,' she warned getting up from our table.

In the street I questioned her further about these thugs.

'It is everywhere. Some of my friends pooled all their savings to buy a small restaurant near Nevsky Prospect. Soon a gang came asking for money.

My naïve friends foolishly refused. The gang beat up one of my friends, so badly,' Marina shuddered, 'He was in hospital for six weeks. They had to close their business, and lost everything.'

On another occasion, when we were in this same café, Marina nodded to a side room. In it were six Russian police dining.

Marina whispered, 'They get their cut also'. Noticing my concern she added, 'Don't worry they are only interested in businessmen not people like us.'

I resolved it would be a missed opportunity if I didn't see Lake Ladoga, the largest lake in Europe and one of the largest, fresh water, lakes in the world. I read it holds approximately 48 species of fish and it is only twenty five miles from Petersburg.

Ladoga Lake is huge; 136 miles long, 51 miles wide, and has often played a major role in Russia's troubled history. It was settled, according to architectural finds, by Rus Vikings from Sweden. In 753 Viking long boats came through the Baltic to Ladoga and from there rowed down the Volkhov to found Novgorod. For two centuries their settlement at Ladoga was one of the most important Viking trading centres in East Europe. A Russian folk legend claims that a Viking, named Rurik, came to Ladoga in 862 and made it his capital. Viking burial grounds, found all along the Volkhov River, attest to this. One of them it is believed is Rurik's grave.

My conjecture is, that Peter the Great, knowing these stories, decided it was a good reason why he should build his new city near here and I believe these Viking Rus sagas created in him his love of the sea. He desired to solidify Russian identity where it all began. Sweden, ever since their Viking conquests, had controlled access through the Baltic and as we have seen, Peter determined to challenge them in war.

Probably the one major thing Lake Ladoga is now remembered for is the way it was used to bring supplies, to the besieged city of Petersburg (Leningrad), during Wold War 11. German Field Marshal Von Leeb had ordered that anyone attempting to leave the starving city should be shot. More than one million Russians died, of starvation, in Petersburg, during this awful, inhuman siege.

One way for Russians to bring supplies, to their dying city, was across Lake Ladoga so, during a severe winter, they constructed a railway over the ice bound Ladoga. It became known as the "Road of Life." I find the account of it one of the most moving stories of World War 11. Not only did Russians manage to bring thousands of tons of food, across the lake of ice, to the city but also using the same route managed to evacuate 1.3 million women and children from Petersburg to safety. Yuri, Sveta's father, the kindly Russian who had let me use his flat in Yaroslavl, had been one of those children.

Not just a railway ran across Ladoga's ice but heavy vehicles also ran a truck express to bring relief to Petersburg's starving people. It remains one of the most incredible acts of courage imaginable. During the first few weeks, of this 'Ice Road,' construction, more than forty trucks disappeared beneath the ice.

I wanted to see this enormous, lake for myself.

Lara was back at school, Marina's time limited but she wanted to help me. We journeyed by Metro beyond the suburbs of Petersburg where at the end of our journey Marina flagged down a 'Chastniki'. These are private cars, not licensed taxis, which many people in Russia use. They are cheaper than taxis, not the same comfort of course, but everyone gains from the transaction. A general safety rule, when using them, is there must be just one driver, for your own safety.

A battered, bumpy Lada, stopped for us and we got into the back. Our driver, we soon discovered, had a serious speech impediment and seemed to have lost his vocal chords. When he spoke to us it was in grunting, belching sounds. On my own I would never have understood any word he spoke yet Marina never missed a word. I realised, with admiration that she never ceased to surprise me. Never had I met anyone with such powers of observation, nor anyone, ever in my life, with such a photographic, visual and auditory, memory. In addition, to these qualities, she had an impressive, artistic ability that matched the best I had seen anywhere.

Our Chastniki drove us over dismal, shaky roads, into flat, monotonous, lifeless countryside. The journey took 30 mins. A broken road eventually came to the edge of a rough, boulder strewn, muddy clay area. It wasn't at all what I had expected. I asked Marina to question the driver to see if he could take us, round the lake to see the old churches and monasteries Ladoga is famous for. He grunted, he could but it was such a long way round it would probably add two and half hours more to our journey. Marina didn't have such time to spare so we got out and waved him goodbye. The fare he asked was so small it would barely have covered his fuel costs. Feeling sorry, for this struggling man, I wanted to offer him more but he had gone.

Close by where we were stopped was a shed like, dreary, windswept café. Lake Ladoga, notorious for powerful, unpredictable storms and winds, was fortunately, on this lowering, grey day, calm, though a threatening, heavy sky subdued any confidence. We entered the dreary café for coffee and blinis, (a Russian dish of small pancakes and caviar), and found, not surprisingly, we were the only customers in this run-down shelter.

Coffee over we clambered over a rock strewn foreshore to be confronted with a swamp of mud. We couldn't even reach the edge of the forlorn lake. Beyond the mud we could see a sandy coloured vista of gently rippling indifference. My only consolation I had at least seen it.

To return to Petersburg we found a local bus. It bounced heavily and slowly, and was stopped with just a hand wave from villagers.

After this, depressing day, I was truly delighted to meet up with the irrepressible Lara. We dined, the three of us, on Nevsky before walking Petersburg's peaceful gardens in the evening twilight.

Russia is a place of spotless, delightful parks and gardens where people sit quietly to read, meet and laugh or cry. No country I ever visited has such enchanting places and often I felt a numinous presence in them just as soothing and eternal as in any Buddhist garden.

About the city, near metro stations, there are small street markets that I learned very quickly not to buy from.

'As I told you, we never know what kind of meat it is,' Marina laughed, 'I don't think their meat is from a cow and anyway who knows how long ago it died.'

There are many other markets however that are excellent and reliable ones that specialise. One I visited, large and open air, sold only fur coats, hats, gloves and scarves. There are no taboos about fur among Russians; it is not just fashion but a matter of survival in their harshly bitter northern climate. Furs on sale there were truly beautiful in design and their blend of colours.

Almost every Russian woman has a fur coat and fur hat. To buy them they save for years, putting money aside each week, just for this purpose. When winter darkness shrouds snow fallen streets and the last leaves of autumn have blown on the wind, one of the delights of being in Russia is to see women, on metros, buses, trains or walking city streets, enveloped in their many coloured coats, collars turned up, against winter's icy winds.

Tourist books, I read about Petersburg, rarely mentioned its diverse array of markets. Marina seemed to know them all. One day she took me to a book market in the suburbs. It was the largest book mart I had ever seen, and housed within several, former Soviet, warehouses. At insignificant prices I was able to buy historic volumes of Russian literature, in English and Russian. We spent hours browsing and even then couldn't see it all; there were so many stalls and sellers, surrounded with rows of, sometimes precariously balanced, angle iron shelves.

Everyone's favourite Russian author, Fyodor Dostoevsky, during the last three years of his life had lived in a Petersburg overlooking Griboedova Canal. One fine morning I set off to see this apartment and hopefully feel his presence there. His flat, at number 5 Kuznechny Street, is now a museum. In Dostoevsky's days it was by Russian standards a considerably small residence. Like Tolstoy, and many of the petty nobility, Dostoevsky had been an addicted gambler and like all gamblers forced to live frugally. The museum is in two parts, one a floor of five rooms, where he lived with his wife and children, the other floor devoted to his literary genius and life. In the flat are his personal belongings, his hat, a book of fairy tales, that he liked to read to his children and a child's rocking horse. His desk is there, on which he wrote 'The Brothers Karamazov,' and nearby a painting he admired, 'The Sistine Madonna.' Like his father had been Dostoevsky was religious and often seen in the magnificent 18th century Vladimir Church close by his flat.

Fyodor's father, Dr Mikhail Dostoevsky, a celebrated physician, worked in a hospital for the poor in Moscow. For his services he had been elevated to the rank of 'Collegiate Assessor' which then placed him 8th in the Russian nobility ranking system of 14 elevations. Because of this honour he was able to buy a small estate, 100 miles from Moscow, with serfs to farm it. On his father's side of the family, Dostoevsky was descended from a long line of priests.

When 16 years old Fyodor's mother died and within two years of this event his doctor father died also. At 18 years he was alone. Like many youths, then and now, he dreamed of changing the world. Socialist ideals attracted him and catching the mood of the times, he joined a subversive group whose goals, sought freedom for serfs and changes in Russian law. Twelve of the group, including Fyodor were betrayed and arrested, spent eight months in the Peter and Paul Fortress and were condemned to execution. Tied to stakes, and within one minute of death by firing squad, a horse galloped into the square to tell them Nicholas I had stayed execution. Dostoevsky and his friends were given eight year sentences. Fyodor served four years, in a Siberian prison camp in the most appalling of conditions. He was categorised as dangerous, which he certainly wasn't, and manacled most of that time.

Dostoevsky was described, by those who knew him, as melancholic. When you learn of his painful life, before he was 30 years old, that I think was inevitable; who could smile after it? Prison changed his heart about revolutionists. From non-violent principles he saw they had become people without morals or compassion and, fostered as he had been on biblical ethics and conduct, Dostoevsky no longer sympathised with them. One revolutionary, Sergei Nechaev, encouraged his followers to deny all social conventions and to even murder ones friends. This malignant idea, opposing every fabric of

Russian society, haunted Socialist ideals thereafter reaching its apex in Lenin, Stalin and his Politburo of murderers, torturers and rapists, Further afield this godless principle indoctrinated and seeped into Mao Tse-Tung's ideals in China. Dostoevsky, wanting nothing to do with such evil, continued to advocate reform but wouldn't espouse violence.

Revolutionary ideals that stated, 'the end always justifies the means', percolated into the Russian Psyche and continues still.

In Dostoevsky's flat, come museum, unable to sense this remarkable author's presence at all I left there disappointed. From here I went to see his tomb in Tikhvin Cemetery, close by the Alexander Nevsky Monastery. He and his parents would have been proud to see it there among Russia's great and famous.

I strolled, thoughtfully, through the tranquil, leafy surrounds of the 'Cathedral of Transfiguration' and on to Tauride Palace, home of Catherine the Great's lover Potemkin, another exceptional, extraordinary Russian, then to Tauride Gardens (Tavrichevsky Sad), and Smolny Convent and Cathedral.

Smolny Convent was built in 1748 to educate young noblewomen nearly 200 years before Oxford University would accept female students. In the central area of the complex is Smolny Cathedral, known for its spectacular concerts and superb choir. This lovely area was used by Lenin, in the early days of the Revolution; no humble dwellings for him or his ideas of equality.

Leaving Smolny, uneasy at being alone, I returned home to meet with Marina and the enthusiastic Lara.

Lara's paternal, great grandfather had been a Sergeant who died in the Second World War, and died defending Petersburg. There is a memorial to him in Kirovsk, 23 miles to the east of Petersburg that she wanted me to see.

Marina suggested it was best to go by bus so I could see more of the Russian countryside. We set off, on the one hour journey, sharing a bus filled with irrepressible, jovial Russians in happy camaraderie.

Kirovsk founded in 1929 quickly grew into an important manufacturing city. During the Second World War it became the only entry point for goods crossing, 'The Road of Life,' over Ladoga, to relieve the starving people of Petersburg (Leningrad) during that inhumane siege.

We walked through Kirovsk's, peaceful, green, spacious streets of handsome buildings. The memorial, Lara and Marina wanted me to see, was behind a small, respectfully railed enclosure. Lara stood in silence looking at the inscribed name of her ancestor. He had died in the terrible battles of Nevsky Pyatchok, where between September 1941 and May 1943 some 200,000 Russian soldiers were killed as they attempted to break the Petersburg siege.

A large, diorama museum, has been opened by Vladimir Putin, in Kirovsk, to commemorate sixty years since the siege ended. Soldier's corpses were discovered in this area, by volunteers who set about digging them from the battlefield. A systematic attempt at naming all of them has begun. No one is more proud of their hero military than Russians.

After this visit, the remarkable Lara, wanted to show me also her father's grave, in a remote country village, 35 miles from Petersburg.

'Of course,' I consented.

One grey, weekend morning we set off and after buying flowers, caught a bus heading towards south east Petersburg, a journey of one and a half hours passing through lonely farmland and decayed wooden villages. Our fellow passengers were struggling villagers who, after visiting Petersburg to shop, could hardly afford their fare home. One crafty old lady, signalling the driver to stop, when asked for the fare kept telling him, 'Wait a moment, wait a moment,' then when the bus halted she just exited with her bags, without paying before he could do anything to stop her. I noticed he wasn't willing to do anything about it and smiled. He understood full well her aged poverty and had seen it all before.

The bus, travelled slowly, stopping whenever passengers asked to be put off, or signalled to get on. Eventually we came to a small wood, set in arable fields, at the left of the road, and we got off. In the distance, half a mile away, I could see a community of tall Khrushchev flats and wondered what on earth those people could be doing there, for a living, in such isolated farmland.

Marina, walking ahead led us along a dirt path into the wood to an area of a perhaps a dozen graves. In the grey light of morning it exuded sadness. All the graves were generally overgrown. Lara stopped beside one of them. An enamelled photo of Lara's father stared back at us. The inscription showed he was 30 years old when he died. Marina, placing flowers in the grave urn, showed no emotion but there were tears in Lara's eyes for a father, she had no memory of, who had died when she was one year old. Reaching into her bag she took out a wrapped toffee and placed it on the plinth of the gravestone in a moving act of sad affection. Only rustling leaves disturbed the silence.

Two graves away was an uncle of Lara's father, who had also died when a young man. Showing me the grave Marina told me, once more without any emotion, 'He was stabbed to death in a card game.'

From this poignant, woodland, cemetery we walked an adjoining narrow, country lane until we reached the small, isolated community I had noticed ahead of us. Here were monotonous blocks of flats and only one shop.

Looking at the shop, with disdain, Marina remarked, 'It's owned by a Chechen.'

Russians hate Chechens, not because they are Muslim, but because of their prolific criminal gangs, involved in selling poisonous illegal alcohol, theft and their ruthless drug cartels in all areas of Russia.

Pointing upwards to a fourth tier of windows Marina singled one out and said. 'That is where we lived. My husband was a capable man. He could make anything, very creative, but suffered from severe depression. He took to alcohol non-stop. I had to separate from him. Then one day he was found hanging in his flat. All photos, of him and us, and his passport had been thrown onto a fire. Police believe it was the work of Chechens who, realising their liquor had killed him, tried to make it look like suicide then tried to hide his identity.'

'Did they arrest them?' I asked.

Marina shook her head, sadness transforming her pretty face into that of an aged woman. 'He was a handsome man, six feet four inches tall, slim and broad shouldered.'

Shocked by this account I asked, 'Do you think he committed suicide?'

'The police believed Chechens sold him bad alcohol, a lot of that goes on. They make toxic liquor and sell it cheaply. He had drunk some of it and it killed him.'

At last I began to understand, Marina's cold appearance, the subdued anxiety showing itself, in nervously twitching fingers, when she was alone, and her lack of emotion, which was really a façade to hide behind. Like many Russian women she was deeply superstitious. When alone I noticed she spent hours seeking direction, with cards, and sometimes writing her inner dreams and longings on pieces of paper, which she burned in the kitchen sink, sending them like a prayer to heaven.

We returned to Petersburg, by bus, then dined on Nevsky.

Forgetting the sadness of the day Marina told me, 'My deceased husband's aunt is a famous folklore singer, in Moscow, named Elena Sapocova.' She was proud her husband's family, and her own, had high achievers among them.

'My father, whom I never met because he left when I was a baby, had been born in Volgograd. During the war he had been a Soviet pilot and, in many ways, was very accomplished. He is buried in the Urals in Revda. I was born in Gorlovka in the Ukraine. It was very pretty and green then, not like now.'

When I asked about her present husband Marina, smiling thoughtfully, replied, 'He is a good man, very handsome, six feet two, from a Kalmyk family.' Noticing my uncertainty she added, 'They are the people south of Volvograd, the only part of Russia that is Buddhist.' She said it proudly. 'They were also Cossacks like my own Ural ancestors.'

Taking a photo from her purse Marina showed me a photo of her husband, in his colonel's uniform, standing beside Vladimir Putin. With her husband's military duties in Moscow it wasn't easy for them to be together so they rang each other every few days. He often visited Petersburg to be with her and Lara. On such days I strolled through Petersburg's streets and gardens or visited the tranquil space of Pavlosk Park.

One day I caught my favourite slow train, which stops conveniently near the park, and walked through the expansive Pavlovsk's gate leading to the palace. The air was clean among the trees, squirrels and birds. Pavlovsk's birds, the tamest I have ever seen anywhere, ate from one's hand, even chaffinches. Woodpeckers and nuthatches searched the trees unperturbed by visitors. Pavlovsk's squirrels are red, as they once were in England before the introduction of the bullying American greys.

Renting a dinghy I rowed the park lake before hiring a bike to cycle the extensive estate. Near the palace entrance, a German vendor was selling glass paintings by a celebrated Russian artist living in Berlin. Her work impressed me so much I purchased one from him.

Pavlovsk Park is huge, enchanting, dreamy and tranquil. It is Russia's Garden of Eden, designed to look like an English garden, and the largest landscaped park in the world. Without the austere, grid line, patterns of French estates, it was conceived from the beginning, with winding paths, natural secretive lakes and such wide variety of trees and plants it has become a UNESCO World Heritage site.

One of the finest ideas, of Soviet Russia, was changing these grand Tsarist palace estates into places of public use. Pavlovsk has low levels of pollution because the Soviets meticulously maintained its pristine beauty. Anyone visiting notices its air quality immediately.

The Boy Scout movement in Russia began in Pavlovsk, under its founder Lord Baden Powell. A great bonfire was lit to commemorate Russia's youth joining this international movement. Sadly it wasn't long before ego driven Lenin replaced it with his own, 'All Union Pioneer Movement'.

After cycling and walking, for three hours, I managed to see just a third of Pavlovsk and had no time left to search its woods to glimpse its famous herd of Elk that roam there.

A tree lined river glides sleepy, through the Estate and walking beside it I became sadly aware I would soon have to return to England to meet Russia's visa requirements. There and then I decided, when that had been done, I would return here eagerly.

The following Wednesday came, the day for my departure. It was a late evening flight. That day turned out to be one of the worst I had ever spent in this country I had grown to love.

Russian government employees, and high ranking civil servants, derive perverse pleasure in tormenting even their own people but foreign tourists are a major target. They steal from everyone, when they can and especially tourists. They have become government sponsored thieves and racketeers. I had already seen some of this undisguised corruption seeing Russian police, taking bribes from motorists, allying themselves with protection racketeers and using prostitutes for their own sexual deviation, instead of arresting them or their pimps. I had been a victim of Bolshoi theatre managers, changing theatre seats and pocketing difference in price, but I didn't expect to find criminality at Petersburg's international airport even though in Samara, customs had deliberately falsified the weight of my luggage, to charge me excess baggage. That was nothing compared to what I was about to experience at Petersburg's airport.

Pulkovo airport is owned by Petersburg city. The Governor of Petersburg is a close friend of Vladimir Putin who appointed him to the position of City Administrator, including the airport.

Marina kindly accompanied me by bus. She and Lara waved goodbye at Pulkova customs entrance. After reluctant farewells I promised to return as soon as my visa had been renewed in London.

At check in my passport was inspected by a tall, fortyish, angry, officious looking Russian man and a much older woman. Glancing over my documents the man asked, in excellent English, 'How much money are you carrying?'

'One thousand dollars,' I replied.

'Open your wallet and let me see.'

I opened my blue money pouch and emptied it on the desk.

'We are going to confiscate this. You can collect it from us when you next visit,' the customs bully said.

'No, you are not,' I replied, taking my money back and zipping it in my pouch. 'I will go to the British Embassy if you try to.'

'The British Consul has no jurisdiction here.'

'This is my money, I worked for it, so I am going to the British Embassy.'

'OK,' the reply came back confidently arrogant.

The woman customs officer, who had remained silent all this time, was noticeably disturbed by the conversation and what had just happened. She hurriedly left her desk.

I picked up my hold-all, and suitcase, and walked out of the airport.

After a long day, packing my bags and feeling tired, I was shocked by what had occurred. By now Marina and Lara had gone. It was already dark outside the airport entrance. I found a phone booth and searched, with difficulty, its Russian directory for the number of the British Embassy. My Russian isn't fluent. I tried ringing a telephone operator for assistance. Before I could speak to anyone two airport police appeared and arrested me. Taking me to an office, at the side of the airport, I was told to sit down.

Four policemen then began to interrogate me. Two of them spoke while the other two, threateningly, stood guarding me.

'Where have you been while you were in our country?' I was asked by a calm, deliberate, officer with notepad in front of him.

Taking out my notebook, containing addresses in Samara, Yaroslavl and

Petersburg I wrote these down for him.

Looking at them the police officer asked, 'Do you have phone numbers for the people you met here?'

'Yes,' I said and wrote these down from my notebook.

The other policeman began ringing all the numbers, or pretended to, I had given to them.

'None of these numbers are answered,' the policeman said, gazing suspiciously at me.

'Well they are all valid and one is Dean of Yaroslavl University, one of the others is a Samara businessman. The others are Russian friends, the family of a Russian Army colonel,' I replied, completely perplexed by why I was being treated as a criminal for visiting Russia as a tourist.

Pushing five forms, towards me, the seated officer instructed, 'Fill in all your personal details and addresses, and phone numbers, of everyone you have visited in Russia.'

This I did.

'Sign all of the forms,' I was ordered abruptly.

Looking at the more congenial looking policeman I said, 'I will give you $100 to get me on my aeroplane.'

Gazing calmly at me the officer answered, 'It won't cost you that much, just $40.'

Opening my wallet I gave him the money. He then stood, saying, 'Bring your luggage and follow me.' He marched ahead of me back into the airport.

Leading me to the customs desk, where they had attempted to rob me, he spoke firmly to the bullying Customs official who had refused my entry.

The customs officer still refused.

An angry exchange took place between him and the policeman who demanded sternly, 'Pochemoo, pochemoo, (Why, why)?'

While all this was happening a mature, grey haired customs officer, with silent air of authority, taking a seat nearby suddenly, speaking forcefully, to the domineering customs officer, without even looking at him, ordered, 'Nyet'.

Walking over, the sour faced customs man began to argue, with the older man, who never once looking into the officer's face, replied forcefully again, 'Nyet.'

The obstructive customs bully, shrank in humiliation fell silent and waved me through the barrier. The accompanying policeman walked away with troubled, resentful, stare.

I was surprised that in spite of this interrogation, of one and half hours, the aircraft, I was due to catch, was still there waiting. At last, I thought, but this unnecessary chaos was still not over. At luggage check in I was confronted by a clerk with cynical smirk on her face. She told me 'Your luggage is fifteen kilograms overweight. You need to pay one hundred and fifty dollars more. If you don't pay we will confiscate your luggage until you do.'

My bags, I knew, weighed much less than when I arrived in Russia. I didn't argue, I was so glad to get out of the place. The flight had now been delayed for two hours, with all its passengers on board except me, just because of this bewildering episode. Afterwards, recalling it, I couldn't understand what it had achieved. Why all this aggravation and confusion for a total of $190 of my money, involving airport staff, police and others, that delayed a flight for two hours?

This was just one of many occurrences I experienced or observed in Russia, moments that seemed to have no logical reason, little supervision and hardly any discipline. Once reading a book of Russian fairy tales I noticed the stories had no hidden moral lessons or any folk wisdom that such stories usually convey in other nations. Russian folk tales are colourful narratives. Unlike Grimm Brothers, Hans Anderson or Aesop's Fables there are no underlying meanings within Russian folk stories, they are simply entertainment. They reflect life in Russia, existence without direction. Churchill's famous comment that Russia is 'an enigma' is undoubtedly true, but 'corrupt enigma' be more accurate. It is seen throughout Russia's history, in which everything collapses into chaos, and must be endured by everyone. My conclusion is, Russia remains uncontrollable, illogical and unpredictable.

Back in England, I was dismayed at our lack of personal space; roads so heavily trafficked it took 25 minutes to cover three miles; long shopping queues everywhere; no room to walk on city pavements. Already, in spite of its shortcomings, I began to miss Russia, the beauty of its architecture, art, palaces, monasteries, its great rivers, immaculate parks, everyday kindness and sociability of ordinary people, its excellent transport system, wide streets and clean pavements.

Back home, my door jammed by a mountain of mail, and invoices. I gave myself three weeks to handle these and obtain another visa. To my absolute surprise, a visa was granted within one hour at the Russian Kensington Office.

Thinking the British government should be made aware of how tourists were harassed at Russian airports I contacted the minister in charge. Her reply came back that the Russian Embassy said I had failed to fill in one of their forms on arrival in Petersburg. I replied tersely that, 'I totally disagree.'

Ringing Svetlana in Moscow I asked, 'Would it be convenient to visit you?'

'Well there's certainly much to see here but I can't accompany you I am too busy. If you wish I can find you a better apartment than the one you had in Peters. Just give me one day and I will have it for you.'

Sveta, as always, was true to her promise.

TORTURED CITY

Sitting beside me on the flight to Moscow was a good looking, athletic, man in his mid-twenties. A confident glow on his face, made me think he was in show business perhaps an actor. He told me he was a Russian acrobat, working in a celebrated international circus. His wrists, I noticed before we spoke, were exceptionally powerful. Showing me his business card it had a photograph of him in spectacular acrobatic pose.

The flight passed quickly in conversation. This time I made sure all required documentation had been filled in even though I knew it made no difference to tourist harassment by Russian customs.

Outside the airport terminal an eager queue of taxis, with Russian drivers looking like mafia gangsters, confronted me. They shone with deceptive friendliness ready to pounce on innocent prey. Approaching one I asked a fare to Moscow city.

'Three hundred dollars,' the driver smiled.

In Russian I told him, 'No, too much.'

Surprised, I spoke Russian, he suddenly looked ashamed and uncomfortable. Another driver, looking shabbily unprofessional, rushed over to offer the journey for one hundred and I accepted.

Moscow is one of the largest and most expensive cities, in the world and one of the coldest. It covers approximately 970 square miles and continues to grow rapidly.

It shouldn't have been a surprise to me that my taxi driver kept losing his way. He must have stopped at least three times, to ask for directions from passers-by, to help find the address I gave him in the south east of Moscow.

Eventually, after hours, we halted at a secluded block of apartments, near the spectacular Tsaritzino Park and Palace, in a secluded suburban location with a metro just half a mile away. The building two storey, set back from the road, was surrounded by wrought iron fence and car park

Helping me with my luggage the taxi driver, quite innocently, suggested, 'If you need a taxi while you are in Moscow, please let me know,' as he gave me his phone number. I nodded politely thinking to myself, 'Yes, if I want to get lost some time I will.'

On the ground floor, of the apartment block, a security concierge directed me to two desk clerks. When I tried to pay, using credit card, I was told, 'We can only accept cash.'

Asking, 'Where is the nearest cash machine?' The young woman directed me to shops some 15 minutes' walk away.

The apartment was superb, large lounge, enormous bedroom, spacious kitchen, contemporary shower bathroom and large walk in wardrobe. Furniture was clean, modern, elegant. I couldn't have wished for a better place to stay.

Ringing Sveta, to tell her I had arrived safely, but the taxi driver had got lost, she thought this so funny I could hear her laughing, with her fellow lecturers. She promised to find a day to visit, when time allowed, from her lecture schedules.

The following day I walked to the nearest metro, Orekhovo, an unimpressive, concrete pillared station with few people on its platforms.

Moscow has one of the deepest, and most architecturally beautiful, metro systems in the whole world but this was not one of them. Moscow metros were intentionally constructed deep, to act as shelters during times of war.

When Nazi Germans were close to Moscow in 1941 several metros were used as Russia's strategic headquarters. The deepest of all these amazing places, Kirovskaya (now Chistye Prudy), was used as Stalin's own headquarters. Another chasmic metro was used for planning Russia's anti-aircraft defence.

I decided, on this first day, to visit Moscow's famous Red Square so, with a folding metro guide, I also set off to explore this, world renowned, colossal metro system on the way there. It was like walking through an art gallery. Tickets were inexpensive but I was invariably confronted with the same, endemic, arrogant obstructions, deliberately inflicted by government employees. At one booth I asked, quite precisely, for a ticket. The obnoxious clerk realising I was foreign pretended not to understand. Luckily a woman, standing near me, repeated my request and I was given a ticket but with a raised brow of self-important officiousness. Like government employees, all around the world, Russians seek personal power, over a defenceless public, whether you pay their wages out of your taxes or not but in Russia this kind of bullying has been elevated to prominent heights, a remaining legacy of Stalin, a dictator who under the guise of equality, secretly murdered his friends. Stalin's close Politburo friend Beria not only murdered and tortured thousands of innocent people but was notorious for picking up pretty teenage girls from Moscow streets to rape, murder and bury under the floors of his dacha.

Like enchanted caves, beneath the frantic turbulence of Moscow, metros are places of escape, into a world of endless, chandeliered, statued, marble tiled grandeur. Of all these wondrous metros Revolyutsi (Revolution) Metro is far the most spectacular. Its yellow, red and black marble arches, have on each side full size bronze statues of men and women of the Soviet; farmers, soldiers, factory workers, pilots, animals, all remembered in seventy two remarkable sculptures.

It was Nikita Khrushchev who had overseen the construction of these majestic metros designed as 'Peoples Palaces'.

To view their chandeliered, mosaic and statued halls is one thing but to travel on Moscow's metros quite another. On them the air foul and unhealthy. At times I could hardly breathe in the stale air and often developed a headache after using them. It was a relief to get outside. Travelling on them, in the evenings, I watched Muscovites, who had to travel daily in this claustrophobic, subterranean labyrinth, looking as though they were on their last legs. More than 50,000 people, annually, seek medical attention from effects of the poor air quality of Moscow's metros. Carriages are ventilated by scoops, above them that capture air when trains move. Air enters the metro underground via street vents which results in stale air being circulated between street shafts. The system is being replaced, by more efficient ventilation methods, but with 203 metro stations, carrying 8 million passengers daily, this is an enormous task.

Greater Moscow is a third larger than London and of course metros are the quickest way to travel around this enormous city. Traveling on them gives an opportunity to see how hard the average Russian works. On evening, overcrowded metros, middle aged passengers simply slump, exhausted in their seats; young men and women, with drooping, tired faces, stand in squashed carriage gangways packed to the doors. Guide books describe Moscow metros as being among the safest to travel on but I didn't find that. There are pickpockets sneaking among the exhausted crowded lines of passengers. Once I discovered a razor blade, deliberately pushed down the back of a seat, so that anyone sitting there would have had their clothes and buttocks shredded as well as their back pocket. One late night, descending a metro escalator, I noticed someone had viciously forced a metal side strip inwards towards the escalator steps. It was tearing passenger clothes and legs. At the bottom of the escalator, in a glass booth, was a security clerk watching passengers. On this occasion the woman sitting there was smirking as she watched passengers tear clothes and legs.

One late evening I couldn't get into a metro entrance hall because staff had closed all six doors but one. People were scrambling, forcefully pushing, to get through this one door but the crowd wasn't moving. Pushing my way to the front of the queue I found a struggling man whose thick coat had caught a pocket in the metro entrance door handle. The thrusting crowd made it impossible for him to free his clothes and he was close to being trampled on. Thrusting the crowd back, shouting at them to stop, I managed to free the man's coat. Watching metro staff had done nothing to help, nor did they open any of the other doors. It all seemed wilfully malign.

Once the pleasure of seeing these beautiful metros had worn off I began to hate travelling on any Moscow subway.

To end this first day in Moscow's city centre I found an inexpensive smorgasbord restaurant, with excellent food, and spent an hour there before going home to the peaceful, tree lined, district of my apartment.

Hoping to visit St Basils Cathedral, in Red Square, the next day being brightly sunny, I made my way to central Moscow. It turned out to be a Russian soldier's holiday parade in the enormous Square. It wasn't possible to even cross its spacious grandeur. I watched the marching precision of soldiers in their proudly neat uniforms. Veterans of WW11 paraded each side of the Square loaded with medals and honours. On one old man I counted 19 medals.

Red Square is 500 metres long, and at one end is the imposing red building of Moscow's Historical Museum and at the other end is St Basils Cathedral but not open on this day.

Leaving the proud and showy display of Russia's military pride I walked over to GUM, the largest department store in Moscow. I'd read that, along with stores in nearby Nikolskaya Street, it sells more expensive designer clothes than Paris, London or Rome combined. That gives some idea of the wealth of Putin's Russia.

GUM a world renowned historic building has three arcades, sheltering beneath a curved glass roof and like everything in Russia has endured a turbulent history of change. The imposing 800 feet façade was built 1890-93 but GUM existed as a store long before that. Originally, it had been commissioned by Catherine the Great, and known as, 'The Trading Rows', a mix of 1,200 stores which, during the Napoleonic invasion, in 1812, all went up in flames. After Communism eradicated the grandeur of Imperial Russia the restored structure was converted into offices for one of Stalin's committees. When Stalin's troubled, sensitive wife Nadezhda killed herself he displayed her body for all to see in GUM. The store eventually reopened in 1953 and is now in private hands.

GUM is more than attractive, with its elegant, expensive shops, wealthy clientele and walkways of wrought iron bridged under a glass roof which in winter allows light to fill the arcades with a softened, snowy glow. There are fountains, tropical plants and seats on which to lounge the time away from Moscow's withering winter.

After tiring of Gum's splendour I visited an area known as the Arbatskaya.

Arbat Street, close by the Kremlin, is pedestrianized and since the fall of

Communism, has become one of the most desired streets to live on in Moscow. Dating back to the 15th century it is one of the oldest streets in the city and once the main road to Moscow. Now traffic free, it's a touristy street of stalls, cafes, and restaurants.

At number 53, Arbat, Pushkin once lived in what is now Moscow's Pushkin Museum. When he married, his famously beautiful, unfaithful wife, he rented this mansion for them when it was a street of artists, poets and academics.

Napoleon's occupation, of Moscow, led to the destruction of many of Arbat Street's old mansions. At the rise of the Soviets many Kremlin officials lived here and now, since the fall of Communism, it has been much renovated. On sunny days, such as the one when I visited, it is a delightful place to see, with street artists, souvenir sellers and pleasant places to enjoy coffee, sitting outside just people watching. You never know what famous Russian will stride by. In late afternoon sunshine I dined there, just before one of the tempestuous rainy deluges, Moscow is known for, began to harass street markets and tourists. Returning home I got lost on Moscow's complex metro system. Even local Muscovites do this. Eventually tired, and soaking wet, I reached my apartment and stayed home for the rest of the day. Rain was so torrential, that evening, there was nothing I could do. Like Petersburg summer rains, in Moscow, appear in minutes, angrily bucketing, to cloud and darken city streets, and often pass just as quickly.

The next morning, the storm had gone to reveal a clear and bright, cloudless sky. Off I set, once more, to see the Kremlin fortress in Red Square. Walking across the great parade ground, to the entrance, a security guard told me I could not enter that day. The whole of the Kremlin was closed that day for a film production.

If cities have their own consciousness and life I surmised Moscow didn't want me there. To be honest I didn't want to be there either. Of all the cities I've visited, round the world, this one was is my least favourite. Somehow all of its once great beauty and fate filled history has been spoiled. My lingering impression was of chaos and confusion. Its magnificent architecture had been ruined by Communists; its wonderful churches despoiled and its incredible metros a place to die in of debilitation.

In this vein St Basil's Cathedral, didn't disappoint either. Constructed in 1555-61, during the reign of the serial killer Ivan IV, (The Terrible), whenever I saw this structure it reminded me of Walt Disney fairy tales. Its origin is so obscure there are several accounts of who built it. According to folklore it was built by an Italian architect and when completed was considered so wonderful the Tsar had the architect blinded so that he could never see or build anything more beautiful again. Another story tells it was designed by two Russian architects, the most likely conjecture, because there is no way an accomplished Italian architect would have created this monstrously comic building.

On entering St. Basil's I was astounded at the high nave, 156 feet. Surrounding it are nine chapels, and everywhere brightly coloured murals glare within its claustrophobic, narrow galleries. To reach these numerous chapels you must climb a confusion of stairways, like clambering inside a medieval fortress.

St Basil's has changed names three times, quite common in Russia, eventually being named after St. Basil, (The Holy Fool), because his bones are interred here. To be extremely holy, in Russia, was known as being a fool for Christ said to happen to saints from reading too many bible texts, in other words they became, 'So heavenly minded they were of no Earthly use.'

Red Square and Kremlin, Moscow

St Basil's Cathedral, Red Square, Moscow.

Memorial Flame inside Moscow's Kremlin.

Dormition Cathedral, 15th cent, in Moscow's Kremlin.

Whomever the architect of the Cathedral was, I concluded he was most certainly mentally deranged, like Ivan himself. I climbed the Cathedrals narrow stairs to see its tiny chapels.

Stalin had wanted to demolish St Basils, as he had done so many other Cathedrals, but after a revered Russian architect objected Stalin left it standing but put the architect in prison for five years.

You don't need much imagination when looking at Red Square, with its Kremlin and St Basils, to notice immediately the contrast between Kremlin fortress, with all its horrific history of cruelty and oppression, and the strange Cathedral creation over the tomb of a holy man of gentle purity. It undeniably reflects an unresolved duality lingering in the Russian mind and nation as a whole.

For just a moment I thought of visiting Lenin's Mausoleum, with its embalmed, mummified, Soviet leader on display but decided the idea too macabre to even consider. The Mausoleum, designed like a Pharaohs tomb, has Lenin's name over the entrance. I couldn't imagine any other modern nation contemplating such a thing. Lenin like Stalin, Beria and Khrushchev was after all just another mass murderer of the Russian people.

In the evening I attended the Bolshoi Ballet and this time had a seat in the stalls, to watch a performance of Tchaikovsky's Nutcracker. I wasn't cheated out of my seat here by some government employee, as I had been in Petersburg. That doesn't however mean the Bolshoi Theatre in Moscow is less corrupt or the staff more honest. During its recent six year renovation there have been allegations of fraud and embezzlement. The government owned project, ended up paying an estimated 1.1 billion dollars, instead of an estimated 380 million.

Bolshoi Ballet Company, the largest in the world, employs 200 dancers and it is true these renovations have made the building a spectacular opera and ballet theatre with dramatic lighting and a computer controlled stage that can elevate to three tiers to allow designers to be more innovative.

The first Bolshoi theatre was begun, in March 1776, when Russian Prince, Ourousov, and an English businessman Michael Maddox, founded it. Like many Moscow buildings this theatre burned in the flames of 1812 but was soon rebuilt.

I sat, in a red velour seat, next to a pretty unaccompanied woman to whom, during interval, I took the opportunity to speak. Shaking my hand she told me, in perfect English, she was a medical doctor from Novorossiysk, a Russian port, on the Black Sea.

Accompanying each other outside, after the performance, the woman told me, 'My name is Tamara. I am not Russian I was born in Poltava in the Ukraine. Poltava's a beautiful old city but I can't go there anymore, too dangerous. It's sad because my mother still lives there.'

Tamara was about 50 years I estimated, with the same purple blue eyes I had noticed with Svetlana, who also is part Ukrainian.

'Would you like a coffee?' I asked.

Smiling, Tamara agreed, 'Yes OK but I don't know Moscow well, I'm only visiting my daughter who works here. We hardly ever see each other, we live so far apart. The hospital I work in is very strict about giving time off.'

Over coffee, Tamara asked, 'Can we meet tomorrow? We are both on our own and I can't be with my daughter because she's working. What do you think.'

I was grateful to have someone so pretty and intelligent to share the day

With, 'Marvellous,' I agreed, 'My Russian is inadequate and it will be a pleasure.'

The following day we met and decided to visit Gorky Park, named after Maxim Gorky, the celebrated Soviet writer. On the banks of the Moskva River, Gorky was wasteland until, in the 1920's, the Soviets created a park here for the people. Over the years it began to take on the appearance, not of greenery and a place of peace and reflection, but one of cheap untidy fairground café stalls and booths. In winter the park floods, as though an unremitting Moskva River would like to wash it all away forever. Undeterred, Muscovites ice skate its numerous, frozen paths between fairy tale icicle laden, frosty trees.

With its undeniable shabbiness, Gorky Park developed a reputation for crime. In 2011 this dishevelled rundown litter of a place became unacceptable in the new Capitalist Russia. Renovation began by clearing out its cheap stalls and Gorky is now one of the leading theme parks of the world, with boating, roller coasting and a gigantic 15,000 square metre ice rink. During winter it is beautifully lit for skaters, blading and gliding, down its tree lined paths. In summer it is filled with sunbathers and picnicking families. There may be serious corruption in Moscow, but there is also massive improvement and this new park is one of them.

Arriving at Gorky you are confronted by enormous, pillared, entrance gates. We looked forward to a day of amusement. Hardly a hundred yards into the park my phone rang and it was Svetlana.

'I am in Moscow and free for the day. Can you meet me at an art exhibition?'

'Of course,' I assured, glad to see her again and that was the end of our visit to Gorky.

Sveta, meticulous in professorial detail gave us metro locations and precise directions. We arrived one hour later to meet. Inside the exhibition building we drank coffee before viewing its modern paintings and other art. Afterwards Svetlana, who had arrived by car, took us to see the reconstructed Cathedral of Christ Redeemer.

Russia had been deeply religious from the 9th century when Byzantium sent missionaries to Kiev after which, for a thousand years, Russia was bound to the Orthodox Church. Subversive Soviets however replaced these ancient ways with Godless atheism. Strangely, Stalin in his youth had planned to become a priest then in a complete transformation, like a dark angel, he destroyed religion and created a new ideal with its Saviour Lenin. The Russian soul was not so easily converted and, beneath all the terror and horror of Stalin's dictatorship, Russia's people remained quietly, secretly religious and in times of panic even Stalin called for prayer.

After Russia defeated Napoleon in 1812, Tsar Alexander I decided to build the tallest Cathedral in the world, 335 feet tall, on the banks of the Moskva River to commemorate this iconic victory. It was begun under Tsar Nicholas II, in 1839, and took more than 40 years to complete. When finished it covered a massive 8020 square yards with five domes, all gilded and one with a diameter of 100 feet. It was a giant Cathedral clothed in white marble. Inside it dazzled with grey, white and red stone, its walls were covered with murals painted by Russia's most famous artists. Light entered its immensity from more than sixty windows and its interior was lit with 4,000 candles. It was estimated 7000 people could worship there, and this lovely Cathedral could be seen, dominating the landscape, from the very walls and secret halls of the Kremlin.

Stalin had already destroyed many churches considering them a waste of valuable space in his own designs for a new Soviet Moscow. This Cathedral of Christ the Redeemer fell too. In its place Stalin planned to build, 'The Palace of the Soviets', even taller than the destroyed Cathedral and this time a giant statue of Lenin, the Saviour of Russia, would sit atop the new building. This madness was stopped in its tracks, after the former Cathedral had gone to rubble, with the threat of Nazi invasion. Stalin now realising the unifying purpose and strength of religion requested Russia's people to go to Church again, to pray for deliverance. There weren't many churches left standing, after Soviet vandalism, and Muscovites thought it another trick to arrest them.

After the collapse of Communism Russia decided to rebuild Cathedral of Christ Redeemer and more than one million people donated money to raise it once more, and revive it as an even more massive place of worship, this time to hold as many as 10,000 believers.

Russia's churches are again filling to the doors with Orthodox Christians. Both Dr Svetlana and Dr Tamara, my companions, were devotees and regular attenders at Church.

The new Cathedral is filled with tourists, wondering at its revived traditional art work. I didn't find an atmosphere of holiness nor the enchantment I often feel in old Russian churches. The place dampened my spirit. For me the whole of Moscow, not just this Cathedral, breathes like a malevolent fog emanating from the soul of Stalin and his unimaginably evil politburo.

Noticing my mood Sveta took us to a favourite Japanese restaurant for lunch then dropped us at Tsaritzyno Park, the Palace estate near my apartment. All Russian parks are scrupulously maintained. We strolled past floral displays, a lake and over classical bridges to view the palace. Many grounds men were Siberian Kalmyks working silently ignoring visitors. We found a first class restaurant, in the park, and left when it began to rain.

Invigorated by the peace and beauty of Tsaritzyn Tamara and I met again the following morning to explore it further. This magnificent estate, begun in 15th century, over the years had been owned by the most prominent nobility of Russia. Catherine the Great seeing it, in 1775, was so impressed by its fertile meadows she bought it. The palace which now dominates the estate was built at her command. The result is majestic, with woodland paths, bridges, large lake, several churches, a museum and great fountain brilliantly lit at nightfall. There are Slavic burial mounds here that are 900 years old.

After strolling the Park we set off home to wait for Sveta and her daughter Kate, who had journeyed from Yaroslavl just to meet me. They thought we should visit another favourite park, near Sveta's home, on the Moskva River, facing the Kremlin.

Kolominskoe Park, a country estate of the Tsars, was an Imperial favourite until Peter the Great's move to Petersburg. All Russian Tsars, before Peter, preferred to live in wooden palaces. Tsar Alexis had built a renowned wooden palace at Kolominskoe. Catherine the Great had it demolished but fortunately there were drawings of it in architects documents and it has been rebuilt. This incredible wooden palace had been covered with carvings coloured blue, green, red and gold. Inside it reflected Western ideas in décor and furniture. Tsar Alexis, who marvelled at mechanical objects, had a throne in the Palace with moving mechanical lions each side of it. Alexis' son, from his second marriage, was Peter the Great who as we have seen inherited a similar fascination with mechanical objects.

Walking through this beautiful park, with its steep banks above the Moskva River, was a genuine delight. As time for evening mass approached Sveta rushed us to the estate's church in time to see its sanctuary doors opening to reveal a gigantic painting of Christ's ascension. Erected in 1532, to celebrate the birth of Ivan the Terrible, the church is built of white stone and is unusual in having a tent spire instead of a Russian dome roof.

There are two other old churches in the park, the Church of St John the Baptist, erected in 1547, and Church of Our Lady of Kazan, erected in 1650. Peter the Great's log cabin is also here, brought by the Soviets from Archangel. The original wooden palace, with its maze of corridors and 250 rooms, has now been reconstructed; work on it began in 2010.

Kate, Sveta's daughter, was tired from her long journey. We sat at a wood table, in sunny, evening light, facing the Moskva River below us, to drink Kvass. This was to be, though I didn't know it at the time, the last time I ever saw any of them.

Saying goodbye, I walked the evening with Tamara, who recited for me one of Shakespeare's sonnets and did it so beautifully and emotionally, in her gentle expressive voice that I have never forgotten it. Shakespeare is a popular favourite in Russia, a country where poetry has always been revered. Often I sensed spoken words, in Russia, carried far greater weight and meaning to the individual than anywhere else I had been.

Next day, waking to a sunny morning, Tamara met me and we set off to view the Kremlin once again, for the third time, hoping we would be lucky enough to get in.

Behind its tall red walls the Kremlin is an enormous fortress of Palaces, and Cathedrals, as well as a seat of government. Long queues, slow moving, stretched ahead of us to its entrance gate. After one shuffling hour we finally reached it. A tall, cold, poker faced, security guard took my passport and asked 'German?'

'Nyet, Anglichanin,' I replied.

'Oh! You're alright.' The guard answered, in perfect English, waving us into the fortress.

There's an old Russian saying that says, "There is nothing above the Kremlin but Heaven, and nothing above the Tsar but God," and certainly Russia's Tsars held the greatest of authoritarian power over their subjects. In the 13th Century approximately 30,000 craftsman, as well as military, Church leaders, Russian nobles and their families, all lived within these formidable walls. Peter the Great, who hated Moscow's military, and violent Boyar nobles residing in the Kremlin, changed all that. He left Moscow to build his own city, Petersburg, away from them all and for protection created his own regiments.

Inside this ancient Kremlin Tsars were crowned, and married in 'The Cathedral of the Annunciation', and at death were buried in Kremlin's 'Archangel Michael Cathedral'.

In this, prison like, red fortress noble women lived in isolation; not in a harem exactly but almost, subjected to lonely seclusion, within an area known as 'The Terem'.

When a Tsar searched for a bride he sent scouts, to all of Russia's villages, looking for the most beautiful of women. To hide your daughter, from the Tsar's men, was a punishable offence. Young women were rounded up like cattle, to be inspected, and viewed by the Tsar, who then chose 500 of them, slowly reducing this number, by selection, until one was found. These beautiful, unfortunate, women were merely breeding machines. Russian people said it would be better to throw your daughter into a river than have her selected for these marriage marts.

The Kremlin, revived under Stalin, is once again the official residence of the President of Russia who lives, when there, in the former Terem Palace. Photos show the Terem a truly spectacular place but photos are the nearest you can get it as it is not open to the public.

One could write a volume just about the Kremlin and it would be a horror story. I think it a strange destiny that Stalin chose not Petersburg, but Moscow's Kremlin as his residence and that of his own Soviet elite because from there, just like Tsar's before him, he and his politburo cruelly destroyed many innocent people. Khrushchev claimed hundreds of thousands were murdered, simply because they disagreed with Stalin, or offended him with a glance. This was a place where people were, without cause, executed, tormented and humiliated, all within walking distance of one of the finest Cathedrals in Russia. Nowhere has evil and good, ugly and beautiful, stood so close together as here. The Kremlin's history stains, its readers, with an unresolved sense of confusion. I once read that, "Confusion is where Satan dwells," and if that is true you will find it here. From the moment I walked through its gates I intuitively knew I wouldn't like Moscow's Kremlin in spite its historic splendour. Some areas, normally open to the public, were closed on the day we visited. Tall military guards were stationed, silent and immovable as statues, in detached lines to prevent any entry. I noticed Tamara, a sensitive, spiritual person, was also quietly uneasy within these Kremlin walls.

The Kremlin's Palaces, and Cathedrals, are truly splendid, like walking through a 3D work of art. You would need a week at least to fully experience it all. Outside of one Cathedral, Ivan the Great's Bell, the largest bell in the world, weighing about 200 tonnes stands alone, with an enormous piece of it broken off. This also seemed to me allegorical of Russia itself.

Within the blood red walls of the Kremlin, Orthodoxy held even greater power over the Russian people, even more than the Tsars, themselves subject to Church belief and practice and in slavery to its doctrines. Orthodoxy dictated "all art must be devotional," hence all those religious frescoes, and icons, seen everywhere throughout Russia.

Outside, the diabolical Kremlin, life was one of hard labour. Russians were chained to the service of nobility and on days of respite were chained to prostrations, prayers, and gesticulation dictated by the Orthodox Church. Russians were slaves, both physically and spiritually and the reason Bolsheviks declared Atheism their state religion.

Unconvinced of its grandeur, Tamara and I were happy to leave and we wandered off to Arbatskaya, to drink coffee and stroll its streets of vendor stalls.

'Do you think life was better under Communism?' I questioned Tamara.

'It had its good points, but no one was happy. It made us distrust and hate each other.'

'And now?' I queried.

'Now, we all want to leave, go west, to live in real democracy. My daughter wants to go to Israel because it's democratic, has good education, a warm climate and more opportunity. I want to go to England or America.'

I left Moscow and was happy to do so.

Marina, in Petersburg, reserved the same haunted flat for me. Tamara, with typical Russian hospitality, insisted on accompanying me to the airport. There she gave me a gift.

'Till we meet again,' she said.

She was such a honest, charming, companion I felt sad at leaving her. Our taxi had shown up late. In the airport terminal I hardly had time to catch my flight or chat with her over coffee. We just had time to say goodbye and as happened always with Russian friends we never met again.

RUSSIAN WINTER

On crowded bus and metro, from the airport, I reached Petersburg to be met by Marina and Lara who, laughing in pleasure came and hugged me. After the dismal chaos, of Moscow, I was pleased to be back in Peter's and in Victoria's haunted apartment.

Winter was beginning to close in and days were much colder. Marina's mother decided to visit, from the Ural Mountains, and stayed with us at Victoria's enormous flat. The journey from Urals by train, a distance 1200 miles, had taken 3 days. Unable to afford sleeper accommodation Marina's mother had slept in her seat and lived off packed sandwiches. Russians, uncomplainingly, accept these long journeys, with Stoic endurance, as part of life in their vast country.

Emily, Marina's mother, like many Russians of her generation, had experienced a troubled life. She had fallen in love with a Soviet pilot who then abandoned her on the birth of Marina. In her teens she had been sent by the Soviets to work in Donetsk in Eastern Ukraine, the place she met and was abandoned by her pilot lover. After spending unhappy years there she was sent to work in the Urals.

'Ural is a bad place to live,' she told me, 'lots of poverty and crime.'

I grew to like this tough, no nonsense, quietly determined woman. Emily was visiting Petersburg not only to see Marina and Lara but because her other daughter had recently died there.

'She just began losing weight. Doctors couldn't find out what was wrong with her. They took her to hospital but she died there without any medically known reason.'

Unable to show any emotion Marina looked on without comment.

Many Russians, I am convinced, die of sadness and melancholy. Marina's first husband had been in this category, living a life he thought without hope, and as a consequence suffered depression.

We visited the cemetery in Petersburg where Marina's sister was buried. In all our many conversations, Marina had never once mentioned to me her sister had died and I'm sure because she was trying to hide from it. Emily went to the cemetery's chapel alone to pray grief plain to see shrouding her face close to tears. Often, while she was with us, she would go out to walk alone drawn into the sadness of loss.

To cheer her, as best we could, we visited a grand, expensive, restaurant in a West St. Petersburg Hotel, that was a recognised venue for wealthy businessmen and 'New Russian' elite. The restaurant had an evening of dance and music. Present were a group of eight, dark suited, sartorially elegant, slim Japanese businessmen. In contrast sat silent groups of dour looking, Russian entrepreneurs, scowling suspiciously as threatening as a Soviet execution squad.

Our table glowed with laughing and loud voices. Russian women are attracted to Japanese men by a belief in their reputation for hard work and business acumen and see in them an opportunity to escape Russia. At a table near ours they kept eyeing the Japanese table, over their shoulders, hoping for a welcoming glance.

Marina's husband showed up quite unexpectedly, on a flying visit, but didn't have time to join our party, even though I suggested it. Marina went to spend time with him for an hour before he had to leave.

'He is a good man,' Marina assured me. Emily raised both thumbs in assent.

Life in Russia's military isn't easy, the time away from ones family, low pay with little incentive, is one of the reasons many officers leave and turn to guarding businessmen, from protection racketeers or to become gangsters themselves.

When night had grown old, and we were tired of dancing, we walked beside the Neva to gaze at the bright lights of Petersburg's great palaces gleaming across the wide expanse of river.

In our taxi home I asked Marina's mother what life was like in the Urals.

'The towns are very poor, almost slums, they are worker towns. In winter it is very cold,' she answered.

'Sometimes minus 30 to 50. Once I had to walk several kilometres, when I was a child of eight, through heavy snow, in a temperature of minus 50 and on my own,' Marina joined in.

Emily looked downcast at the memory. 'It is all work, nothing to do afterwards, but we do get together on weekends, especially in summer.'

'Couldn't your husband Peter come?' I enquired of Emily.

Emily looked away, her shoulders drooping in defeat. 'In Russia we work very hard. Petra, was coming home and just collapsed from overwork. He is more or less an invalid now and can only take fluids and soups.'

This explanation didn't surprise me. I had already seen passengers, on Russia's evening Metros, tired and completely exhausted. I had never seen such toil worn depletion as I did on these trains and metros.

After a one week stay with us I was genuinely unhappy to say goodbye to the hardy Emily, whose life story had been as dramatic as a film noir.

Winter was near, leaves had fallen, nights came quickly and sadly. By

December temperatures dropped to minus 26C. I soon learned never to go out gloveless, if I did pain in my fingers made me want to howl as fiercely as the wind. I wore a Swiss border trench coat, made in Italy, padded and belted and under this a thick, woollen, roll neck sweater. Sudden snow storms assailed the city unexpectedly and fell so heavily visibility was down to ten yards. It fell, so coldly, I had to place my fingers across my numb frozen brows.

Marina took me to a market, where I bought a fur hat and, fur lined, leather flat cap with ear muffs. It became essential to wear fleece lined trousers and ankle length boots over long woollen socks. On freezing snow days I wore a scarf to cover my mouth with. I was often astounded at the ease with which Russians endured these temperatures; how they adapted their way of walking to avoid the kind of frequent falls, I often had, on icy pavements. In all my time in Russia I saw only one other person skid off his feet and he probably wasn't Russian.

Enchanting, expensive, colourful fur coats and hats, adorning Russian women on every freezing, winter street, and on metros, charmed me. In Petersburg's store windows I saw fur coats priced at $3,000-$4000.

Noticing me looking at fur snuggled women on a metro one evening, Marina explained, 'We save money every week, from our their teens, until we have enough to buy a fur hat and coat.' Marina had never had enough money to buy one of them; soldiers, teachers, lecturers and government staff are paid such minimal wages, often delayed due to corruption at the very top, that many public employees struggle daily.

Cold temperatures, during these short sunless days, I believe, are the reason so many Russians have such healthy, unblemished, and quite often unwrinkled skin.

Winter nights parks, alongside Petersburg's city streets, are an absolute wonder, serene beneath silent snows, glowing under starry, moonlit skies. I often walked Petersburg, on such nights, to drink coffee, visit parks or browse Petersburg's most famous book shop, Dom Knigy. Once there I heard a CD being played, of a Russian girl group singing over the bookstore loudspeakers, I asked Marina, 'What is that piece of music?'

'It's called, "I Want a Man like Putin." They say Putin himself commissioned it to be written and played over all radio stations. He loves to promote himself as superman,' Marina replied cynically.

Now summer tourism was over it became a time for me to observe the way Russians lived. I was surprised at the affluence of the people of Petersburg. Cafés, restaurants and clubs were filled every evening.

Petersburg's winter metros became fascinating with their variety of people. I never saw violence on them, of the kind I saw in America and Britain. One major difference was seeing vendors, allowed to walk through carriages, selling novelties and postcards.

For Petersburg's homeless, orphans and runaways, winter metros are places of warmth and sociability. On ice bound streets streets where metro vents expel warm air into the sky vagrants sleep beside them during cold winter nights.

Extreme cold, during Russia's winters, makes everyone tired and I soon learned to close my eyes during these winter days, to rest and conserve energy, the way Russians do whenever I sat on buses or metros.

Marina was so aware of all around her I often, silently, wondered about her knowledge of Russia's criminals, and Mafia gangs, so I queried her unrevealed life. One of her friends, she told me, had married a Mafiosi. Marina seemed to

228

Moika Canal in winter, Petersburg.

Ice on the Neva River, Petersburg.

Kite Skiing on frozen Baltic Sea.

Winter River Neva, Petersburg.

Atlantes, New Hermitage, Petersburg.

Typical, Russian Winter, Fur Coat.

admire these criminal gangs. Another friend had married a man later imprisoned for murder. She divorced and remarried this time a policeman, and surprisingly both of them, the former wife and new spouse, visited the murderer at his prison.

Marina was also familiar with Russian politicians, perhaps because of their corruption and criminal connections. She showed me a photo of her second husband standing beside Putin on the steps of a government building and it left me leaving me wondering whether her husband was a part of Russia's FSB.

No matter how many times Russian women marry, in their romantic heart, there is only one man they long always to be with again. This conclusion was drawn from listening to Marina, Marina's mother, Sveta in Yaroslavl and Galina in Samara, all of whom had fallen in love, with someone in their past, that they looked upon as the only true love in their life. Another characteristic is their extreme, passionate jealousy of such intensity of the kind I had only noticed in Spanish speaking countries.

Marina told me she had only loved once, a boy she met when at college, and since then just endured all other men. My impression was she hated everyone, except her daughter Lara. Marina was always isolated, lonely and introspective, and I often felt sorry for her.

In Petersburg suburbs I sometimes saw gangs of young gypsys, all small in stature, dark skinned, dressed colourfully, moving rapidly through streets, or up metro escalators, like packs of wild dogs. Marina, held tightly to her purse, and shoulder bag, whenever they appeared. These swiftly moving gangs disappeared as quickly as they came, like flocks of silent birds.

At minus 26C the River Neva was frozen. I went to its banks expecting to see it flat like an ice rink, instead it was a splintered chaos, of broken ice, as jagged as broken glaciers. Neva ice is torn by shipping and re-frozen into impassable gigantic shards. Several guide books said that when the ice breaks on the Neva it can be heard all over the city.

'Have you ever heard it,' I asked Marina.

'I know people say this but, in all my years living here, I never once heard it. It's like an urban myth. Maybe it was like that hundreds of years ago.'

With the delight of frozen rivers and lakes fishermen take to them with circular wooden disks, to which they attach a drill to bore into the thick ice to lower their lines. Once I saw one of these fishermen carrying his wooden disk and drill, slung across his shoulders, travelling on a metro.

Russians never hide away from their wonderful winters. Snowfall isn't a time for sorrow, or sense of loss of summer, but a time of rejoicing. Russian winters are truly, endearingly, unforgettably beautiful.

One minus 26C day I walked beside a wide stream, in the outer suburbs of Petersburg. In spite of the brittle cold, dazzling sunshine dappled its way through cotton wool clouds and suddenly I found myself enveloped in tiny ice crystals, falling all around me, in a fairy glitter of diamonds reflecting the rays of the sun. It seemed like some mystical experience and I have never forgotten the enchantment of it.

Like an artist snow contrasts everything into fine lined shapes. On these cold days I enjoyed walking the city observing the magic of parks in snow and delighted at seeing women wrapped in their colourful furs. Russians have always, historically, dressed more creatively vibrant than anyone else on earth and modern Russians continue this tradition. Searching paintings and glancing through Imperial era photos of Russian dress, spanning its enormous empire, I am captured by the creativity and exuberance of their rainbow colours.

Evening nightfall is just as enchanting. One late evening, beside the Neva, I came across a floating restaurant, a tall ship schooner, encased in thick coat of ice, frozen solid in the river and sparkling with hundreds of decorative lights across its masts, booms and deck.

One afternoon, in a street off Nevsky Prospect, I came to a shop side door entrance enveloped in eighteen inches of transparent ice caused by water from a leaky overflow pipe and thought it beautiful. This cloak of snow, and ice, everywhere is like walking through an alluring fairy tale.

In this winter wonderland Victoria's haunted flat continued to create problems for me. Russian homes are heated by State owned central suppliers. All over Petersburg, in this coldest of winters, the hot water supply failed. With Marina's help I purchased an oil heater, which did little to alleviate the extreme cold of the flat. Improvising, we stuffed paper in all window gaps. This hardly made any difference either and most evenings, before bed, I sat huddled over our useless oil heater. That winter, of minus 30c temperatures, many older Russians died of extreme cold. Often when walking past flats, in Petersburg suburbs, I noticed inch thick layers of ice inside, not outside, apartment windows.

One brightly sunny day Eva and Lara journeyed with me to the shores of the Baltic. The sea had frozen as solidly as the Neva in the extreme cold. People were skiing, tugged by huge kites across the ice of the Baltic as far as the horizon.

We walked confidently, adventurously, across the frozen sea.

I hadn't learned the Russian skill of walking on, ice glazed, frozen streets and often fell, once so badly I injured my right wrist. I never saw Russians fall they have an acquired ability of walking straight with equal distribution of of weight from one foot to the other.

In winter Russians not only ski the frozen Baltic, but also enjoy their snowbound, interminable forests, with hunting, snow mobiling and cross country skiing.

During these months Nevsky Prospect, and adjoining streets, divert everyone with music venues. Restaurants and cafes become a riot of revelling and winter haven every evening. On light-starved weekends, churches and monasteries glow cheerily with candles, filled to capacity with genuflecting worshipers. They are enchanted places, even outside of winter mass, to be alone with one's own inner peace.

Before the Soviet era winter was always a time of festival happiness. In the 17th century Russian Tsars, wrapped in grand Russian coats, travelled by horse drawn sleighs, followed by courtiers, going from house to house singing carols. Right up to 1917, close to Xmas, streets were brightened by carol singers holding their candles and bright stars of Bethlehem.

No one celebrated Xmas like Russians did, in the dark days of winter. There were visits to families, kin and friends all dressed in their best, magnificently coloured, clothes. Winter was also a time of elaborate feasting, and fasting, days when families came together devoutly to celebrate, because in Tsarist times Russians were a sincerely devout people. Anyone reading Orthodox prayer books quickly notices the ideals of purity and celebration of love for each other that Russians once aspired to.

On Neva ice, people of Petersburg, each Epiphany on 6th January, built a church filled with Bibles and icons. A hole was drilled into the river to represent the Jordan stream where Jesus had been baptised. A Priest lowered a cross down this opening, into the river, for mothers to baptise their babies.

All over northern Russia, slides were made from ice for children, and adults, to rocket down. Ice Forts were built for children to play in and on frozen rivers there were sleigh rides that skated the ice like dancers. Empress Elizabeth, Peter the Great's daughter, once built a huge ice mountain, complete with slide, 50 metres long, topped with a golden cupola, 80 feet high, attached to which donkeys pulled revellers to the top of this mountain on sledges. For all nobility, and estate owners, winter became a time for troika sleigh rides and partying.

Soviets destroyed all that.

Near Xmas, two of Marina's friends came to visit. Olga, a Siberian in her late thirties, accompanied by a six feet four, heavily built, dark haired, handsome Swiss named Bernard. They met, Olga told me, while travelling around Russia. Like many Russian women Olga was sexually a free spirit. I could see this propensity troubled her sensitive, introverted, religiously inclined friend who was obviously in love with her but Olga so sure of herself, was nevertheless cruelly determined to be promiscuous.

'We were travelling on a sleeper train, from Lake Baikal, and met some young Americans. Olga just decided to sleep with one of them, in my compartment.' Bernard, downcast, told me.

When I stared quizzically at Olga she said, 'Well he was a very handsome man, so why not.' She, arrogantly glanced cynically at Bernard, deliberately tormenting him.

Marina suggested we all go to a nightclub, which we did. It was to a second rate hotel filled with women but few men. There was a bar so I ordered drinks for us all. In an adjoining room was a lively sounding disco.

A young, pretty, blue eyed, Ukrainian woman drinking at our table told me, as she stared into my eyes, 'Ukrainian women are considered the most beautiful in the world.'

Marina, overhearing, joined in and said, 'Why don't you sleep with him?'

Laughing at them both I drank my wine.

Olga disappeared into the disco by herself. Marina rose from our table, holding Bernard's hand, to join the dancers. I didn't wish to dance, just listen to the music, filtering from the other room as I enjoyed my wine. Greeting their return, with uplifted wine, I admired Russian instinctive companionship and familiarity.

BIRTH OF A NATION

Russia was born in Novgorod, not Moscow, not Petersburg, so I decided it was time to visit this World Heritage site.

Novgorod, 104 miles south east of Petersburg, has no buses that reach it during winter, due to heavy snows. The only way would be by train but one travel agent offered a winter tour of three days, hotel included, to this ancient city, so I booked a place.

The morning I left it had snowed heavily during the night. This didn't deter the tour operator at all and the coach left, on time, from Ligorsky Prospect Metro station. I was surprised to find every seat booked. The dilapidated coach seemed decades old but the seats were comfortable. A Russian guide, a woman in her late fifties, sat near the driver.

Russia maintains its roads diligently, even in the harshest of winters. In defiance of the deep snow banks each side of it the road to Novgorod was open.

Hamlets and small towns of wooden houses, from Tsarist days, floated dreamily passed our windows. Everywhere seemed quiet, deserted, and forgotten. I supposed these villages were mostly lived in by older people, snuggled beside their stoves, or by absent 'New Russians' who came only in the summer.

Our journey took four hours to complete, at a rickety pace of 25 miles an hour. Eventually we stopped, beside the frozen, snow banked, River Volkhov in countryside outside the medieval city. Our Soviet era, run down hotel, was shabbily third rate. The room, I was assigned to, was the worst hotel room I

238

had ever been in; small with cheap wardrobe, single bed with saggy mattress, a shower that didn't always work, or produce hot water. In all respects the worst of Communist period establishments.

When I asked a hotel receptionist, a typically disgruntled Russian woman, for a better room and reasoned I would pay any extra cost, she replied, 'All rooms are taken.'

Later I found Russian nationals had been given the best rooms and foreigners the dingy ones. Western press often mentions Moscow's Kremlin corruption, in reality corruption runs throughout Russian society, from the highest political peak to the lowest trough of society. Nevertheless the hotel was in a superb location, surrounded by open countryside. Beyond, the snow bound landscape, across the Volkhov river, I could see the splendid domes of venerable Novgorod, a half mile distance away. The late afternoon air was penetratingly cold, the sky light grey and the river a broken plank of ice. In the distance, veiled by winter blue mist, I could just make out Novgorod's Kremlin red walls and peaking above them the shining, golden, onion dome of St. Sophia Cathedral.

That evening the tour operator provided a banquet for us all, with bottles of vodka, ending with a night of dancing. It was an excellent dinner, during which I had a chance to meet some of the other tourists. Sitting opposite my chair was a thirtyish dentist with his wife, from Petersburg, who when they thought no one was watching put spare bottles of vodka into their shoulder bags.

At the end of our sumptuous meal, the tour operator came looking for missing vodka supplies. She knew guests had all been presented with one vodka each and some had definitely gone missing. When asked I answered that

I didn't even consume the one placed in front of me. A woman, sitting close by, quietly informed the guide the dentists had stolen them.

Surprisingly no one got drunk, after drinking these bottles of vodka. When tables, and centre floor, were cleared, a band began playing rock, and disco music, to which I joined in dancing. Late in the evening, rough looking, local men, not from our tour, came in to join the dancing so I went off to my rickety bed early.

Novgorod is one of the most ancient of Russian cities. It was here that Swedish Vikings settled, with their lord Rurik. It became the centre, with Kiev, of the 'Rus,' from which Russia takes its name.

Vikings, generally portrayed as marauding, fearsome plunderers, were much more than that. They were sophisticated warrior traders who with skilfully designed ships could sail wild seas or navigate shallow rivers. Wherever they settled they created exceptional art and a cohesive, disciplined society. The wide slow rivers of Russia were ideal for their longboats and trading ventures. From here they could trade with Greece and Byzantium, and is a reason they established their centre at Novgorod.

Lake Limen, close by Novgorod, fed profusely by rivers, drains towards Lake Ladoga to the north which in turn gave Vikings access to the River Neva and Gulf of Finland. These numerous river systems allowed them to sail their elegant boats to the desired wealth and trade of the Mediterranean.

Lord Rurik was probably Swedish but no one knows for certain since Vikings were from all over the Scandinavian north. Rurik, it is believed, founded Novgorod in 862 though some Russian manuscripts show it settled as early as 859 perhaps by his Viking scouts.

Novgorod soon became one of the first true Western democracies ever to be

Founded and Rurik's Viking descendants thrived to become a dynasty that ruled Russia until the 17th century.

The full name for Novgorod is 'Veliky Novgorod' to avoid confusing it with Nizhny Novgorod, a Volga River city, built much later in the 13th century.

Lara's paternal family all originated from Novgorod. I had noticed, the moment I met her, Lara's Scandinavian appearance. Marina, of Ural Cossack Bashkir descent, looked entirely different from her daughter. Photos of her Lara's father, before his tragic death, show a tall, sandy haired man of six feet four inches, broad shouldered and slim that agreed with my assumptions and recent DNA tests have shown that the present day inhabitants of Novgorod still carry Viking ancestry in their blood.

Novgorod a World Heritage Site, has 604 historic monuments within the city and surrounding area. Among these are 26 of the oldest churches in Russia and it is believed the iconic onion dome of Russian churches first appeared in Novgorod most likely copied from Byzantium.

This astonishing, timeless city became one of the greatest trading centres, of Europe, with established links to Asia. As it grew so did its enlightened democracy. Novgorodians governed their region with a council, 'The Veche'. They met, when occasion made it necessary, by the ringing of a city bell sounding solemnly, like a call from God, across the wild, vast plain of their domain.

The day after our arrival we assembled to visit the ancient city but since our tour guide could only speak Russian I set off, to explore alone, with a guide book in my shoulder bag.

Novgorod's Kremlin walls were originally of wood, as were those of its famous St. Sophia Cathedral. A wooden fortress was built around the rapidly growing city, in 1044, stone towers were added in 1302. Grand Prince of Moscow, Ivan III, became so envious of the enormous wealth and success of Novgorod he annexed the city and built the magnificent Kremlin we see here today.

Ivan 111, known as 'Ivan the Great, Grand Prince of all the Rus', due to his expansion of Russian territory, was fearsome, tall and thin with naturally curly hair. It was said his wild staring eyes caused women to faint in terror. In jealousy in 1470 Ivan marched on Novgorod.

Novgorod had much to be envied for, not only its enlightened democracy and wealth, but also because it had become a renowned seat of learning. One of the most notable rulers of Russia, Yaroslav the Wise, had founded a school for 300 pupils here, in 1034, in this most prosperous of all cites. There is a Russian folk tale about it that tells of one of its merchant traders, named Sadko, who owned thirty ships that sailed Novgorod's Volkhov River to Lake Ladoga and from there to the River Neva and on to the blue sea and Constantinople, the Queen of all cities.

Success often attracts envy, and jealousy, that ends finally in destruction. The famed wealth and prosperity of Novgorod couldn't last nor escape the centuries of turbulence Russia had endured. Even worse was to come with the accession of Ivan IV, (The Terrible, 1547-1584), who, envious of Novgorod's success, suspected them of defecting to Lithuania.

Ivan the Terrible, mentally deranged, swung between bouts of devout religiosity to soulless, horrifying acts of cruelty. Compulsively paranoid, one day he turned his malignant attention to Novgorod at a time when in 1570 Novgorod was enduring a devastating plague that killed 10,000 people. Ivan thought this time of misfortune an opportune moment to attack the great city. To do it he used his personal military bodyguard, the dreaded, demonic Oprechniki.

The Oprechniki had been formed in 1565 to report any evil, heard or seen, that criticised Tsar Ivan. This armed bodyguard can only be described as the most diabolical military regiment, and brotherhood, ever imagined. Dressed in long black robes, riding black horses, they carried an insignia that showed the severed head of a dog, and a broom, that told everyone they were there to sniff out treason, in word or deed, and sweep it all away. Their unfortunate victims, were mocked before being inflicted with depraved cruelty; boiling victims alive, tearing limbs off using horses attached to each limb and sometimes impaling their prisoners to roast over slow fires.

Leading these soldiers from hell, on 6th January 1570, Ivan appeared outside of Novgorod, in the bowels of winter cold and darkness to exact his kind of satanic assault on the city's unsuspecting inhabitants. His first act was to verbally denigrate the Archbishop of Novgorod, who had come to meet him. Then, in his bewildering evil derangement, Ivan asked to go to divine service, in St Sophia's Cathedral, as though to thank God for the evil he was about to unleash on Novgorod's unsuspecting citizens.

After this act of maniacal worship Ivan began humiliating clergy of all Novgorod's Churches and monasteries before plundering their treasures and icons, from the surrounding districts. Innocent Clergy were arrested and flogged for one whole day, unless each paid Ivan 20 roubles. Novgorod's own Archbishop was arrested and imprisoned.

Ivan's bodyguard tore down monastery bells and destroyed whatever they could find, even church livestock. Twenty seven of the oldest monasteries in

Russia had their treasures stolen, including St Sophia's, where Ivan had prayed before destroying the city.

Middle and lower class citizens suffered most from Ivan's madness. Whole families were arrested to be tortured in the most vicious way, roasted on grills or hung by their wrists and eyebrows burned off. Women, and children, were bound and thrown from cliffs into the icebound Volkhov River where, if they rose to the surface, they were pushed back under the ice, with boathooks and lances.

In all, around 200 landowners, 100 servants, 45 officials, and their families, were murdered. Shops and warehouses were destroyed; homeless and paupers expelled from the city, to die of cold and hunger, outside the city walls. An estimate, of people murdered, is set at approximately 7,250.

Once this demented devastation had been accomplished Ivan's men followed it by destroying ninety per cent of Novgorod's surrounding farms to make the terrifying subjugation complete. This massacre at Novgorod lasted five weeks. From that time onwards the once magnificent, birthplace of Russia irrevocably declined into provinciality.

Every Tsar, since Ivan, has maintained a brutal secret police, including the Bolsheviks. Lenin established his dreaded Cheka to spy on everyone, everywhere. Later Stalin created the NKVD, administered by the weak looking, serial rapist and murderer, Lavrentiy Beria. Putin it's reported has a similar secret organisation within his National Guard.

As though all of that misery wasn't sufficient, during World War II, Nazi Germans occupied Novgorod to engage in their own, customary mindless, ravaging. Of Novgorod's 2,500, historic buildings, less than 40 of them escaped ruin by the end of the war. Russian pride however has seen many of these old buildings restored.

What we have left, of old Novgorod, is still one of the most wonderful of medieval cities to be found anywhere in the world.

On a bitterly cold morning our tour coach drove across the Volkhov. We were dropped off at Novgorod's Kremlin, its great walls banked steeply with snow drift. Entering through the wide fortress gates, at this time of year in the middle of a severe winter, and deep in snow, Novgorod seemed a lonely forgotten place.

St Sophia's Cathedral, with its white walls, silver domes with central one coloured gold, has an austere design. It's incredibly sculptured bronze doors, the 'Magdeburg Gates' were stolen from the Swedish town of Sigtuna in the 12th century.

Inside, the Cathedral is covered in frescos and icons, to the very apex of its domes. There is a 16th century, elaborately carved booth that looks like a confessional, in which Russia's Tsar's sat and prayed. It is a disconcerting reminder that religion is so often accompanied, by extreme cruelty. I speculated whether mad Ivan had prayed in this same beautifully crafted cubicle. He certainly had prayed here, in this Cathedral, before his terrifying massacre of the city's inhabitants.

Just as in St. Basil's Cathedral in Moscow I sensed no holiness in St. Sophia's. Its frescos and icons seem to stare, and watch, like some heavenly Oprechniki or an inhuman court of justice. Hitler's guillotine would not have been out of place beside them. The 12th century iconostasis in the Cathedral is one of the oldest in Russia.

In the centre of Novgorod's Kremlin is a sculptured monument, 'The

Millennium of Russia Memorial', erected in 1862 to mark one thousand years since founding of the city. Even in winter snow it looks a remarkable work. The memorial is surrounded by a waist high iron fence. On top of the monument is a sphere on which stands a figure, representing Mother Russia, kneeling before an Orthodox Cross.

Surrounding the sphere are historic heroes of Russia, Rurik, Peter the Great, the first Romanov Tsar, and below all them are one hundred of Russia's celebrated artists, writers, statesmen and princes.

Hitler had his envious, acquisitive, gaze on this majestic monument that displayed the birth of Russia and its remarkable achievements. His intention had been to dismantle it then rebuild it in Berlin to show German Fatherland's superiority over the Mother of the Slavs. What a mistaken idea that was. Russian soldiers instead decimated eighty per cent of Germany's military might and the monument, to Russia's achievements, remains in Novgorod.

One of the finest historic museums, in all of Russia, is found within Novgorod's Kremlin, just across from The Millennium of Russia Memorial. Its remarkable collections date from the earliest foundation of the city.

Outside St Sophia's, are an array of bells, on brick plinths, rescued from Novgorod's destroyed churches.

Leaving the group, I walked outside the Kremlin and beside its snow bound walls and nine impressive towers. Novgorod's walls and towers are formidable; the tallest tower is 126 feet high. In more clement weather it is possible to walk these city walls on a wooden walkway.

Novgorod city, outside the great Kremlin, has approximately thirty four historic churches and monasteries but I was tired of seeing their architecture and soulless interiors.

In 'The Church of the Transfiguration', there is a fresco of 'God the Almighty' depicting him as a madman with wide staring eyes. If you were to see it in your sleep you would know this was a nightmare. The artist monk was perhaps thinking of the brutality encased within Novgorod's history and saw their Orthodox God as maniac.

The exteriors of these old churches are often magnificent. I was fascinated by the 15th century aspects of 'Church of St Peter and Paul', and 'Church of the Holy Trinity in the Monastery of the Holy Spirit', and many more too numerous to mention.

You might wonder why there were so many churches, and monasteries, in Novgorod. The answer is, even Tsars believed themselves subject to God and Church discipline. Russia's Orthodox Church held all in controlled subjection, as tyrannically as Russian nobles held serfs in slavery. Creativity, freedom of thought and artistic expression was suppressed unless it fell in line with Church Orthodox teaching. For the rest of Europe this was a tragedy since few nations were more creative and intellectually perceptive as Russians. To make matters worse many Tsars were deeply religious, not just Ivan the Terrible, so authoritarian Orthodoxy pursued its religious enslavement and with immoveable traditions subdued any thought of democracy. Not even the reforming Peter the Great felt able to oppose them.

The pendulum of life in Russian history swings often between extremes of holiness and hideous atrocity.

Novgorod in winter is an enchantment of snowscape. Peace falls as gentle as the snow on its architecture, delightful restaurants, museums, cafes and river walks.

Outside the Kremlin, undeterred by the bitter cold, vendors were selling to tourists, some items I thought would sell well in England especially skilfully crafted wood carvings, paintings and sketches.

Returning to the Kremlin I visited the 'Museum of History, Architecture and Art', and it is one of the most fascinating museums I ever entered. Its collections, recalling life in Novgorod from 11th century onwards, includes, household items, armoury, archaeological finds, clothing, sketches, paintings, birch bark correspondence, musical instruments, toys, icons and religious artefacts. Some treasured exhibits are, a gold chancel cross inlaid with precious stones, a Church chandelier of gilded silver and a liturgical, gilded silver, chalice once used at mass. The craftsmanship is so remarkable I doubt if anyone today could produce them.

Birch bark letters in the museum reveal a surprisingly high level of literacy among these early Russians, even within small villages, surrounding the Novgorod autonomy.

Novgorod and Kiev were the first cities to begin recording the life and history of Russia and though many of these historic documents were destroyed, during Novgorod's turbulent 1000 year history, some have remained and this Museum has a rare collection of them.

Among its 12th to 17th century icons is one of the rarest in Russia, 'The Virgin of The Sign' reputed to have brought divine intervention to save the city, during the 12th century, when four Russian princes had allied to capture Novgorod. The story is one that has held the imagination ever since. The origin, of the icon, is not known but it was always kept in Novgorod's 'Church of the Transfiguration.' The story tells that when Novgorod was attacked, by these hostile princes, Archbishop Ivan, of Novgorod, began praying for victory from the siege he knew was coming. While in prayer he heard a voice telling him, 'Go to the Church of the Transfiguration and take the icon of the Virgin from there and show it to the opposing armies'. The Archbishop obeyed this angelic voice and, facing the enemy, held the icon in his hands as he displayed it from the walls of the city. The attacking armies stared at the icon and it began to weep. At this, miraculous event, the Army of Novgorod left their city to attack their enemies and won a decisive victory.

When I saw this old, revered icon, depicting a pregnant Virgin, I was captivated by the compassionate gaze emanating from the Virgin's eyes. There is indeed a compelling aura of holiness about it.

Novgorod's icon artists were renowned for their skill. Painting in bright colours, rather than the customary subdued monotonous tones of the time, Novgorod's artists were known as men of holiness. They fasted and prayed before painting any of their esteemed icons. It is this genuine religious fervour that makes their art so appealing and their icons so valuable today.

Medieval Russians celebrated, and partied, with wandering troubadour musicians. Some of their musical instruments were discovered in Novgorod and give some indication of the sounds of their music. Among them is the oldest known Russian musical instrument, the Gusli, a stringed instrument, of five to 12 strings, played flat, across the knees, like a zither, and is so ancient no one knows the date of its origin. Greeks, in the 6th century, captured Slavic prisoners who were carrying them. A similar instrument, named the Guslim, has been discovered in Sumer, the most ancient civilisation known in Mesopotamia.

In this museum too is a forerunner of the celebrated Russian Balalaika, called the Sopeli, which, like the Gusli, is still in use today among Russian folk musicians. Two other instruments on display worth seeing are the Gudki, a

Russian flute, and a Vargany an instrument much like a Jews Harp.

I would like to have heard these wandering minstrels, with their zither sound, flute, balalaika and Jews harp, to have heard them playing instruments accompanied with their deep, resonating, Russian voices. Slavs have always been accomplished musicians, and song writers, and Russia has some of the grandest choirs anywhere on Earth.

Another museum, if you wish to know how life was in Imperial Russia and well worth a visit is 'Vitoslavlitsy Open-Air Museum of Wooden Architecture' one of only three such museums in the whole of Russia.

With their abundance of wood early Russians realised it was not only more aesthetically beautiful but also better suited to their damp and cold climate than stone. Wood is warmer to the touch, is not subject to condensation and is easily assembled. A Slavic dwelling could be completed, with communal effort, within one week. By the 18th century Russians had conceived a prefabricated way of doing it. You just told a local wood merchant the number of rooms you required and these were then made to order and quickly assembled on site.

Vitoslavlitsy Museum has twenty six, original, Russian wooden dwellings, churches and a windmill. When I visited, in the snow, it was a journey back in time to Tsarist Russia. In the summer, I read, it was even more enjoyable with folk musicians and dancers, there in traditional, kaleidoscopic costumes.

One of the beauties of old Russia was its wooden churches. Some of them are preserved at Vitoslavlitsy. Prince Vladimir, the Viking, born 958, had been a devout pagan worshipper, building shrines and idols all over Russia's north. He must have been the epitome of Viking virility, chroniclers claim he had 600 concubines and many wives. In 988 he converted to Christianity after searching all the known religions of his time. Discovering Byzantine Christians were the most successful, and prosperous, he reasoned that meant favoured by God.

On becoming a convert he made a statement to his subjects, 'Wooden churches should be built, and established, where pagan idols once stood'. Thousands of these magnificent churches were built across Russia's northwest and excavations have found pagan temple stones beneath these wooden church foundations. These lovely old churches, still found in remote Russian districts, are mostly empty now and falling to ruin. I had seen one, near Samara, with its old bell, still in place, hanging silently in its wooden tower and with doors locked this once revered wooden structure was falling into disrepair. Before Communism these holy, lively, inspiring churches were vibrantly colourful filled with frescoes, paintings and icons.

Luckily in a few places they are still maintained in good repair. The Vitoslavlitsy Museum has some of them, taken from northern Russian villages, and reassembled. The oldest is the 'Church of the Nativity' dated 1539, and another is 'Church of St. Nicholas' which is 17th century. In their time they must have been spectacular glowing with brightly coloured interiors and iconostasis.

At the museum even more surprising are the grander peasant houses re-erected here. Some are enormous and invite a re-think of how villagers lived in Imperial Russia. Not all peasants were poor and it's inaccurate to think they were all struggling farm labourers or clod-hopping serfs. Many were superb craftsman, metal workers, carpenters, wood carvers, cabinet makers and traders. Some were so skilled they came to the attention of the Tsars.

Inside, their wooden dwellings, there was a large family room with wide benches, around the inside walls, that served as beds at night; a huge stove for

Novgorod's Kremlin Walls.

Novgorod Kremlin and St. Sophia Cathedral.

252

Tsarist period Wooden Church.

Tsarist period Timber Cottage.

cooking, and heating, and above the stove a place for the elderly, and children, to sleep in warmth during Russia's severe northern winters. There was a large dining table, sometimes in a separate room, and always there were icons, in a corner, for daily prayer. Birch-bark baskets, shoes and utensils, were hung on walls. These cottages are so appealing I would gladly spend my days in one of them instead of our modern characterless boxes.

Russians are innately sociable. Village wives preferred to spin their linen on a portable distaff, rather than use European spinning wheels, because these distaffs could be easily carried to a neighbour's cottage, or be used outside, where on sunny days all met and span together.

Externally these captivating dwellings had colourful window shutters, above which were decorative carvings. There were wooden supports, protecting walkways, and these also were carved and neatly trimmed.

Everything seemed so perfect, but what I didn't see was the smaller peasant cottages that Russian artists of the time sometimes recorded. From this museum, I conjectured, it wasn't possible to learn how the majority of serfs in Russia actually lived.

The Museum guides are dressed in the colourful costumes typical of Imperial Russia. Nowhere did any nation dress so elegantly or brightly, even the poorest of them, as so many artists have shown. Russians have if not always a holy soul then certainly an artistic one above all people.

There are many misconceptions about Russia's serfs. It is true they were bound to landowners but not in the sense of American slaves. Some serfs became extremely prosperous as these, more superior, cottages confirmed. Liberal minded nobility sometimes gave them their freedom, and some enlightened, kindly, landowners helped serfs improve their lives. It is also true some landowners were harsh, notoriously ill-treating their serfs. In severest cases serfs rioted but Russian law always protected the gentry.

Upward mobility for especially talented villagers was possible. Some became revered actors, dancers, musicians and singers and some renowned artists of exceptional skill gained them entrance to Russia's famed, 'Art Academy' in Petersburg. Some serf women were so beautiful their landowners married them. The most famous, of these enchanting women, was the wife of Nicholas Sheremetev, the richest man in all of Russia. Sheremetev, known as a benevolent landowner, held two million acres of land in 17 provinces and employed 210,000 serfs.

Not just Russia but all of Europe at one time practiced serfdom, of a kind, even England. The difference in Russia was reform of the system came too slowly until a tide of change built such momentum that it swept all before it like a tsunami just as it had in France.

Forty tumultuous years before the American Civil War, with its promise of abolishing slavery, there were unsuccessful attempts to end serfdom in Russia. In 1825 a youthful group of progressive aristocrats and landowners, with 3000 soldiers to support them, met on a cold December day, beside the famous statue of Peter the Great, demanding an end to serfdom as, "Our national disgrace," and asked for a constitution.

Tsar Nicholas I called out his Imperial guard and with his cannons the slaughter began. Innocent ideals of progress bled into the squares of Petersburg.

Serfs had their own hierarchy and some chosen to attend on aristocratic landowner families, as overseers, stewards, butlers and entertainers. The most talented, performers, were sent to private theatres of their aristocratic owners.

Count Sheremetev created a theatre of more than 200 serf actors, musicians and artists. He fell deeply in love, as mentioned, with one of them, Praskovya, who had joined the Sheremetev estate when age 7 years. While there she was taught foreign languages, music and singing. Praskovya grew to become a prominent soprano, of such charm and beauty Nicholas Sheremetev married her. She became Countess and bore him a son but she died soon after of tuberculosis. Sheremetev never recovered from the loss, the love of his life, and he himself died six years later.

One of the most celebrated male actors in Russia, Mikhail, had once been a serf. From this acting success he earned enough to purchase his own, and his family's, freedom.

Not all serfs were so fortunate. The laws of Russia didn't permit killing serfs but owners could legally beat them. Russia was so large, incidents were often too remote for any help to be given. Ivan Turgenev, the Russian noble, and famous novelist, had a wheelchair bound grandmother who strangled her serf, boy servant, to death without any charge being brought against her.

Serfs, enduring ill treatment, had a saying, "God is in His heaven and the Tsar is far away." These harshly treated Serfs hardly ever, until the 19th century, rebelled because the Orthodox Church taught them a passage from the Bible, 1 Peter 2:18,

"You who are slaves must accept the authority of your masters with all respect- not only if they are kind and reasonable, but even if they are cruel."

The Tsar, and landowning nobles, were happy to approve such a teaching since they claimed, "God is the Great Father and the Tsar the Little Father".

Nobles and estate owners, who ran into debt, could mortgage their serfs and due to the lavish excesses, of partying nobles, by mid-19th century 66 per cent of serfs had been mortgaged to a Nobles Land Bank. Serfs could also be sold which caused hardship and separation from family and friends. As in slave communities, throughout America, serfs mostly endured this treatment with religious faith.

Among Russians there is a sustaining belief in being part of a large family of "Mother Russia" and it gave gave serfs their will to survive. This belief was encouraged with frequent festivals in which all danced, drank kvass, sang, played music and fraternised and this tradition is still true today. On weekends, Russians meet for family gatherings, in a way rarely seen in Europe. Even when living abroad Russians continue this tradition. I have met Russians who will travel hundreds of miles just to be part of one of their customary get-togethers. They have always been a generous people welcoming all into their homes, to share food, board and camaraderie born out of hardship.

Though some of Russia's nobility resisted reform, serfdom couldn't last.

A young breed of noblemen, educated and well- travelled, pressured for a change that was inevitable. Tsar Alexander II, 'The Reforming Tsar' realising this, on 3rd March 1861 issued his "Manifesto on Emancipation of the Serfs," but, just as in pre-revolutionary France, Russian nobles and landowners objected and this document, that could have saved the Romanov dynasty, was diluted to placate nobility.

Instead of giving serfs total freedom it declared there would be a two year transition period then the land, that whole families of serfs had worked on for centuries, would not be given to them they would have to buy it.

Few serfs had any savings to purchase their land. If they could buy land it would have to be bought in small affordable chunks, not the whole land their forefathers had lived on for generations. Since serfs had little money of their own, the government cunningly offered them 80 per cent loans at 6 per cent per annum over 49 years. In real terms that meant nothing had changed. Serfs were forced to continue working, for landowners, until this debt was paid. Some unproductive farming years left struggling serfs late in payments so Police and Militia were then sent to enforce payment.

How any ruler could have been so feckless and indecisive is difficult to understand. Tsar Alexander had himself told nobles it was, 'better to liberate peasants from above rather than wait till they win their freedom by uprisings from below', yet his manifesto shackled serfs even more securely to the land than ever before and Russia's nobility made themselves an enormous profit at their serf's expense.

The Russian people's response was to attempt assassination of Tsar Alexander. They tried six times over a twenty year period until in March 1881 they succeeded but it still took 36 years before peasants finally won their freedom from below.

Time came for our coach to return to Petersburg. We left late afternoon and it was night by the time we arrived at our drop off. Marina and Lara were there on schedule, waiting patiently for me, in spite of a minus 26 degree temperature. Lara hugged me and took my hand before we caught a metro back to my rented apartment.

My time in Russia was running short. I knew it was time to leave and I was unhappy to do so, it had become the only place I wanted to be. Even if I lived a thousand years this land was so gigantic I could never have seen it all, its beautiful architecture, immaculate expansive parks, cities filled with delightful surprises, its turbulent, courageous history, music and art, its wide eternal landscapes through which flowed, generous, steady, determined rivers that reflected the soul of the nation. Above all I would miss its welcoming, open hearted, intelligent people. There really is no country on Earth quite like it. It isn't perfect, of course, but the only problems I experienced came from corrupt public officials. I felt far safer there than I had ever been in the UK, Australia, or America, or in any of the thirty eight countries I've travelled through. One of the most surprising things was I had seen greater poverty in America than in Russia and professionals there earned far in excess of the ones I knew in England.

Marina needed to be with her husband. I booked my flight back to England to depart the following week. During the few days left together we spent hours wandering winter markets, suburbs of Petersburg, walking its magnificent parks, which even in winter are well maintained and are one of the most beautiful sights in Petersburg. In the evenings we dined at favourite cafes and restaurants and met with Marina's friends to say goodbye.

At Petersburg Airport once again Russian officials, in uniforms of police and customs, attempted to confiscate my money but this time I had Marina with me arguing my corner.

'My husband is an army colonel and a friend of Putin. Why are you doing this? You have no right to behave this way with tourists to our country.'

The Customs official, casting his eyes down, didn't look at Marina but apologised, 'We have to follow guidelines and we have no record of how much money he came in with.'

'He is not a criminal, he has been with my family, and we vouch for him.' Marina spoke determinedly.

The Customs officer, without replying, nodded me through the barriers. I thanked Marina and Lara, hugged and said goodbye.

At the check in desk when I handed over my suitcase, even though I only had clothes in it, I was once more told I had to pay for extra baggage.

Back in England I was dismayed at our untidy streets, overcrowding, train delays and class conscious society. One of the first things I did was join a Russia Club where I could continue to meet these irrepressible people.

Printed in Poland
by Amazon Fulfillment
Poland Sp. z o.o., Wrocław

64234978R00157